THE EMERGENT DECADE

Armando Morales. *Landscape*. 1964.

THE EMERGENT DECADE

Latin American Painters and Painting in the 1960's

Text by Thomas M. Messer

Artists' profiles in text and pictures by Cornell Capa

Prepared under the auspices of the Cornell University Latin American Year 1965–1966
and The Solomon R. Guggenheim Museum

First published 1966

Library of Congress Catalog Card Number: 66-15382
Design by Kathleen Haven
Printed in Switzerland by Buchdruckerei Winterthur AG, Winterthur

CONTENTS

*All text, except where otherwise indicated, is by Thomas M. Messer,
and all profiles are by Cornell Capa.*

LIST OF PAINTERS AND PAINTINGS

FOREWORD

This book is the result of an unusual joint venture undertaken by Cornell University and The Solomon R. Guggenheim Museum. It was conceived as part of the Cornell Latin American Year 1965–1966, a program of conferences and cultural activities designed to stimulate appreciation of Latin America's creative accomplishments and to broaden understanding of its problems.

After preliminary investigations carried out in Latin America during the summer of 1963 by Cornell sculptor Jack L. Squier, the University asked Thomas M. Messer, director of the Guggenheim Museum and a distinguished observer of Latin American art, to undertake selection of paintings for a jointly sponsored exhibition. Mr Messer agreed. In the course of two trips to eight Latin American countries during the late summer and fall of 1964, he made an initial choice of some eighty paintings. These were shipped to Caracas, Venezuela, and placed on public view at the Museo de Bellas Artes and at the adjacent Ateneo de Caracas. This showing, made possible by the generous support of the Fundación Neumann, enabled a sophisticated Latin American audience to evaluate a representative collection of contemporary Latin American painting and greatly facilitated Mr Messer's labors of final selection.

Book and exhibition share the same title. Yet what you are about to read is not a catalog. Neither is it a definitive study. It is meant to be a look, midway through what is clearly a decisive decade in Latin American painting, at the more important art centers of the continent – this through an illustrated interchange of professional views and some deceptively informal, intensely intimate photographic profiles of individual artists by Cornell Capa.

Special acknowledgment for their help in this complex undertaking should go to Professors Squier, J. Mayone Stycos, Steven Muller, and John Mellor of Cornell; Mr and Mrs Hans Neumann of the Fundación Neumann; Mr Miguel Arroyo, director of the Museo de Bellas Artes, Caracas; Mrs Ana Teresa de Otero Silva, president of the Ateneo de Caracas; Mr José Gómez-Sicre, chief of the Visual Arts Division of the Pan American Union; and Miss Linda Konheim, research assistant at the Guggenheim Museum.

Ithaca, New York
January 25, 1966

WILLIAM H. MACLEISH
Director
Cornell Latin American Year

ACKNOWLEDGMENTS

We would like to thank the following Latin American artists and critics for graciously consenting to the publication of their correspondence with Thomas M. Messer: Marc Berkowitz, Rio de Janeiro art critic; Samuel Paz, curator of the Visual Arts Center, Instituto Torcuato Di Tella, Buenos Aires; Jorge Elliott, painter, director of the Institute of Plastic Arts, Santiago; Carlos Rodríguez Saavedra, critic, professor in the School of Plastic Arts and the School of Architecture, University of San Marcos, Lima; Marta Traba, professor of the History of Art, Los Andes University, and director of the Museum of Modern Art, Bogotá; Mathias Goeritz, painter, sculptor, architect, professor in the School of Architecture, University of Mexico.

We also want to thank Clara Diament de Sujo, Caracas art critic, and the editors of *Art International* for permission to reprint excerpts from Mrs de Sujo's article 'Living in Painting: Venezuelan Art Today', which appeared in *Art International* in April 1965.

INTRODUCTION

In 1960, when, as Director of Boston's Institute of Contemporary Art, I undertook a selection of Latin American painting, my intention was simply to put together a good show. Accordingly, I visited relatively few painters, choosing wherever I could their most recent and significant works. The show, presented under the title 'New Departures: Latin America', featured five oils each by Manabu Mabe (Brazil), Fernando de Szyszlo (Peru), Alejandro Obregón (Colombia), Alejandro Otero (Venezuela), Ricardo Martínez (Mexico), and Armando Morales (Nicaragua). Argentina, already in artistic ferment and evidently on the way to establishing a clear hegemony, could no longer be represented by a single painter. I decided to include one work by each of five painters: José Antonio Fernández-Muro, Sarah Grilo, Miguel Ocampo, Clorindo Testa, and the Japanese Kazuya Sakai. The show turned out well. It was of even texture and managed to represent, if not the art of the continent as a whole, at least a selective sample of the mid-generation's most significant work in the countries I visited.

As an exhibition, 'The Emergent Decade' is probably less satisfactory to the eye, merely because the simple and somewhat artificial premise of the earlier show is no longer acceptable. In every respect, we set our sights higher this time. The show is more inclusive geographically, embracing Uruguay and Chile in addition to the countries previously covered. A special effort was made to include the work of the leading expatriates of each nation. More importantly, we deliberately sacrificed even texture (which would have been attainable had we adjusted the selection to an international norm) and emphasized rather than minimized the diversity of art in each country. The result is a very broad stylistic range in which figuration coexists with many kinds of abstraction. Both appear in their expressionist, constructivist, surrealist, and primitive manifestations – to use for purposes of quick identification these general and imprecise terms by which broad categories are described. Finally, the choice reflects a desire to focus on the various levels of creative maturity. In each country visited, I selected works by old masters of modern art, by mature contemporaries, and by the younger experimenters. Each category was treated according to its significance in the whole fabric of a nation's artistic development.

The selection was made in the course of two month-long trips taken to the east and west coasts of Latin America during the last half of 1964. I inspected hundreds of paintings, seeking them out in artists' studios with which I was already familiar or to which I was drawn by the recommendations of other observers, often the artists themselves.

The expenditure of so much time, money, and effort on a purely regional project is unusual in this era of globally oriented museums. Nevertheless, I must point to my endeavors apologetically rather than complacently, for they were clearly insufficient in light of the complexity of the task. When Latin American artists chide us for not coming to grips with the burdensome problems of our common concern, they are only partly wrong. For some of these artists, through their work, propose weighty issues which we have had to approach, I fear, with more sympathy than understanding. Thus, if it is pointed out that there remain countries unvisited and, within those visited, unrepresented painters of importance, I must sadly agree. If, further, it is stated that the media of sculpture and printmaking have been ignored, I must assent again, with the remark that the loss is smaller in sculpture, where works of distinction are very rare though not altogether lacking. If, finally, the objection is raised that the choice is an arbitrary one, my defense may still be only partially tenable. For admittedly every human judgment depends upon the texture, invariably imperfect, of the judge's own knowledge and perception – a texture that may be particularly porous in the area of contemporary art. Arbitrary, however, need not mean capricious. Rather it may signify the isolation of a particular, and hopefully valid, strain in order to illuminate a single area in a great realm of undefined possibilities.

*

When trying to perceive broader currents in art, one always begins by examining individual works. In them we may seek levels of meaning that may be tested further as we move from the single work to the artist's total contribution. But only by studying a great many such sequences can we hope to arrive at a basis for a national or continental style.

The question whether there exists something that may rightly be called Latin American art is relevant to this pursuit. Of deceiving simplicity, the question prompts complex and equivocal responses. To answer in a sentence, Latin American art exists, in some sense, yes and no.

The existence of national and continental identities is self-evident. At the same time, it is extremely difficult if not impossible to render them intelligible by listing their attributes. It is easier to state what Latin American art is not, what it cannot possibly be.

To dispel the most primitive misconception, Latin American art can have no relation to the pictorial sentimentalities manufactured by tourist bureaus. These nostalgic scenes obviously have no meaning and merely confuse by their evocation of a long-discredited myth. Neither, on the other hand, can the essence of Latin America be conveyed other than through a form language that in some way bespeaks the thoughts and emotions, the concerns, problems, and issues, of its origin. An imitative, international style deprived of its indigenous substance will not do this. Therefore, both – picturesque unreality and its opposite, neutral abstraction – must be rejected.

A true Latin American art, if it exists, will be rooted in the realities of Latin American life. If these realities are coherent, their formal equivalents may emerge as a visually identifiable form language. A style, in other words, may come into being. Whenever art lacks such distinguishable features, it must be presumed that coherence either is lacking or has not been articulated in visual form.

The concept of a Latin American art must be rooted in a grasp of the Latin American identity. That identity, however, resists definition. An adequate definition would have to be impossibly comprehensive, for it would embrace geography, history, economics, religion, psychology, politics, and many other factors as well. Reason and emotion, facts and ideas, the past with its memories and its conditioning force, the present in all its fluid immediacy, and an indiscernible future foreshadowed in terms of vague aspirations would all need to be part of it. It would have to be applicable simultaneously to the individual and to the larger entities of family, nation, continent, and world.

Only the artist is equipped to evoke this identity. By means of intuition and by using the implicit language of forms, he is capable of epitomizing the various components of reality. The images he uses are, of course, the products of his own individual awareness and are always relative to a specific content. (One among many common elements of artistic consciousness in Latin America is the obsession with death, expressed in a curious mixture of the Indian and Spanish.) Yet the Latin American artist is committed to articulating not only the legacy of his culture but also those central concerns which he shares, regardless of geography or tradition, with his contemporaries. This simultaneous commitment to a continental frame of reference that is concrete but limited, and to another that is universal and largely unassimilated, produces a field of tension that demands creative release.

In this tenuous balance of superimposed identities, an accurate Latin American profile cannot be drawn in heavy lines. Its visual component, the artist's work, is varied and diverse, and not reduceable to an artificial uniformity. Such a diversity reflects that richness of ideas, of responses, and of perceptions that is as much a part of life in Latin America as it is of life in Europe or the United States. If a subtle unity asserts itself nonetheless, it is a unity that is not inconsistent with diversification, a unity that envelops a fragmented texture with a wholeness that is frail and transparent but nevertheless real.

Conditional recognition of a common denominator should not be taken to suggest that Latin American art is exclusively a regional phenomenon. On the contrary, the Latin American artist is clearly dependent upon the fundamental pictorial modes that hold sway everywhere today. Whatever their origin, the central concepts of our time, whether expressed in words or in forms, provide the guidelines for painters in Latin America, as they do everywhere else in the world. Such concepts are the standard of our age and constitute a legacy that exists whether it is wanted or not. In the end, the problem of the Latin American artist is to find an authentic posture, one that is equally distant from self-conscious isolation and rootless universality.

BRAZIL

Flávio de Rezende Carvalho. *Portrait of José Lins do Régo (Retrato de José Lins do Régo).* 1948.

Mr Marc Berkowitz

Rio de Janeiro, Brazil

Dear Mr Berkowitz:

What I saw in the week that I spent in Brazil was diverse, timely, and interesting, although insufficiently substantial to make the experience consistently nourishing. Both in Rio and in São Paulo, speaking generally, promise outweighed fulfillment, and achievement fell short of an awareness of possibilities. A certain stimulated frustration, therefore, was the inevitable result of my brief visit.

In stating this impression so bluntly, I should perhaps explain that I had confined my attention to painting and that both the graphic arts and sculpture should be ruled out from this generalization. (I passed by a great deal of the former and encountered very little of the latter.) Let me now proceed to particular cases.

The few works by Iberê Camargo that I saw impressed me favorably. He is, no doubt, a painter of accomplishment who leans upon his models (de Staël and Riopelle) without aping their language. One may hope, perhaps, that in years to come his painterly content will become clearer and more substantive, so that he may become something more than a fine painter. Should this happen, then his dependence upon the 'School of Paris' will lessen in favor of a style both more personal and more clearly Brazilian.

Mohalyi and Ianelli, too, are leaning heavily on Paris and de Staël, although we appear to be confronted here with kinship rather than with imitative gesture. This is so not only because the French master's vocabulary is thoroughly adapted to particular and honest creative purposes but also because I found in Ianelli's paintings a startling similarity with de Staël's early work that is hardly explainable in terms of direct exposure. In any event, Ianelli's and Mohalyi's sensitive renditions and skillful adaptations seem valid to me within the limits of their present stylistic confinement.

The painter who, in the end, interested me most is Serpa, who has a great deal of diligent experimentation to his credit. We see this painter, his works neatly arranged in sketchbooks that cover many years of searching, conquering for himself the idioms of cubism and free-form abstraction and taking a good look at Klee in particular. His recent painting reflects an interest in semi-figurative expressionism that may be placed somewhere between the contemporary Spaniards and the early CoBrA manifestations. As one may gather from this particular crossbreed, Serpa's work is not particularly engaging. It may emerge powerfully and truthfully, however, if his current or any future work proves more than just another exercise in the adoption of an existing idiom. His art is still in need of a unifying purpose. It seems possible, however, that its various rich components may be brought together in a comprehensive formal idiom.

On the other hand, Mabe, one of the many Japanese painters residing in São Paulo, seems to have attained unity at the cost of those inventive qualities that marked him a few years ago as one of the most promising painters on the Latin American scene. That dangerous Oriental facility seems to have gotten in the way somewhere and reduced an originally meaningful abstraction to overskilled and mannered statements.

Some of your younger Japanese-born painters apparently sense this danger. Kusuno, for example, creates artificial difficulties against which he allows his skill to flounder. But he is clearly a young talent and his development cannot as yet be predicted. Nor can we be sure about Lee, who is a young eclectic in the linear tradition of Toulouse-Lautrec, Art Nouveau, Klimt, and Schiele. He is clearly gifted and aware of what is going on, which, in view of Brazil's relative remoteness from the world's great art centers, is to his credit. But it is too soon to tell whether we are dealing with a sophomoric game or whether what exists could mature into a full-fledged expression. In the meantime, one may be allowed to amuse oneself by entering into the spirit of his playful work.

There is, then, as I see it from a brief visit, both enough to stimulate and enough to disappoint our ready interest. Many hopeful possibilities are left pending and one suspects that some of the problems comprehended as such by intuitive sensibilities will remain without an adequate formal solution. For what there is, one may well be grateful. Please let me know whether or not you agree with this assessment. As for me, I will want to return in about five years to check these impressions.

Very sincerely yours,
T. M. M.

Wesley Duke Lee. *Valneria. Employee at Marcadium* (*Valneria. Auxiliar de Marcadium*). 1960.

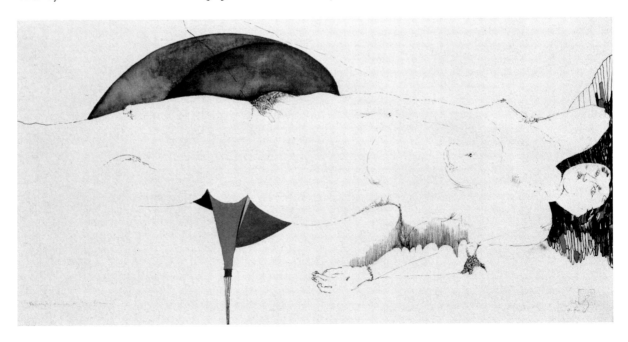

Arcangelo Ianelli. *Gray (Cinza)*. 1963.

Arcangelo Ianelli. *White (Branco)*. 1964.

Wesley Duke Lee. *A Zona: I-Ching*. 1964.

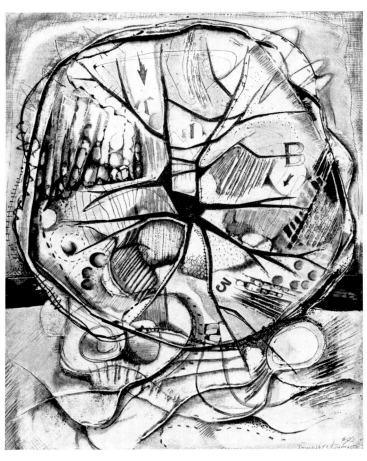

Tomoshige Kusuno. *Civilization of Packages*
(*Civilização de embalagem*). 1964.

Aldemir Martins. *Flowers and Palm Trees* (*Flores e palmas*). 1962.

Iván Serpa. *Birds*. 1963.

Iván Serpa. *Figure*. 1964.

Tikashi Fukushima. *Green Composition (Composição verde)*. 1963–1964.

Wesley Duke Lee. *View of the Doorway and the Forest (Visão da porta e da floresta)*. 1960.

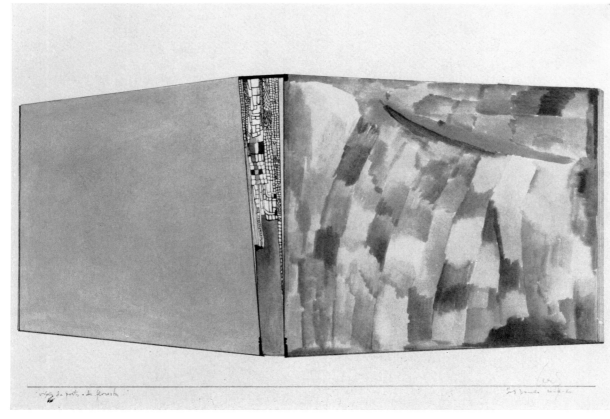

Madrid
April 29, 1965

Dear Mr Messer:

In many instances your opinions on Brazilian painting coincide entirely with mine. You say 'promise outweighed fulfillment, and achievement fell short of an awareness of possibilities'. For saying just this, though in other words, in a foreword which I wrote for an exhibition of contemporary Brazilian art in London and also in an article for the magazine *Studio International*, I have been abused by our artists and by our still very provincial art columns. It is my belief, and I was glad to see that it is yours as well, that only by judging honestly, and by speaking out frankly and constructively, can we render service to the art of our respective countries.

It is a pity, in a way, that you confined your attention to painting, because it is in printmaking that Brazilian art has reached its highest level. Graphic art has now definitely become a movement in depth, and I feel sure that you will find a study of it quite rewarding.

Iberê Camargo is undoubtedly one of our best painters. I have followed his career since 1945, and though he has undergone many influences, he has usually managed to shed them rather quickly. If you see his present work you will notice that de Staël and Riopelle no longer influence him. His style has become more personal, though I don't know that it has become more Brazilian. I confess that I do not quite know what you mean by a more clearly 'Brazilian' style.

In Arcangelo Ianelli's case, I feel more the influence of William Scott. (There was a Scott room at one of the São Paulo Bienals.) Ianelli is about to go to Europe for a stay of two years, and I believe the trip will produce a great change in his painting. Yolanda Mohalyi is also becoming more and more personal in her work, and her color has become looser and more luminous.

Iván Serpa, whom I have known since he began painting, and whose first one-man show I organized quite a few years ago, is really one of my great 'hopes'. Going through many trends, 'isms', and influences, he has acquired a truly outstanding 'metier', and his now completely figurative expressionism needs perhaps only more conviction to make it truly great. And – as you put it – 'a unifying purpose'. But I have great confidence in Serpa's future.

Of the Japanese living and working in Brazil, it is Tomie Ohtake who interests me most. Ignoring the rather facile decorative approach of some of her colleagues, she has matured very slowly. Her present work, superimposed abstract forms worked in depth with an outstanding spatial quality, has attained a very high level indeed.

With regard to Mabe, I think you are quite right. I've said more or less the same thing many times.

Again I agree with you regarding the work of Wesley Duke Lee. It is very well done, but it has a certain slickness that might become an obstacle to his further development.

There are, of course, a great many artists whose work you have apparently not seen – Dacosta, María Leontina, Krajcberg, Volpi, Bandeira, Gustão Manuel Henrique, and quite a few others. I think that they are at least as important as some of the artists you mentioned.

I find it extremely interesting that the North American influence on Brazilian art has been relatively slight, that surrealism has never found adepts in Brazil, that Pop Art – with one or two exceptions – has not yet caught on, and that Op Art had its Brazilian predecessors, though under a different name. Perhaps on your next voyage, you will find time to look into some of these aspects in more detail.

Yours very sincerely,
Marc Berkowitz

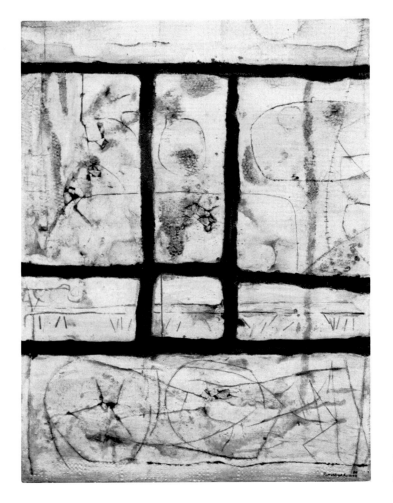

Tomoshige Kusuno. *The Possibility of the Cross.* N.D.

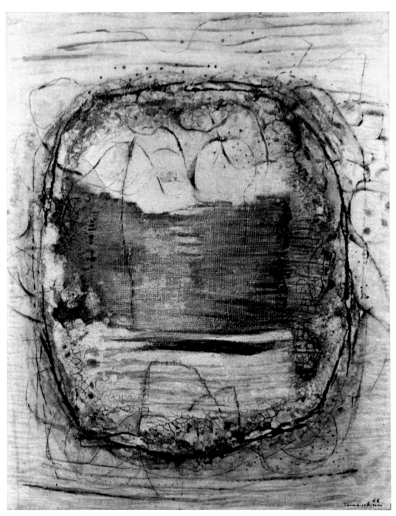

Tomoshige Kusuno. *The Plane in the Circle*. 1964.

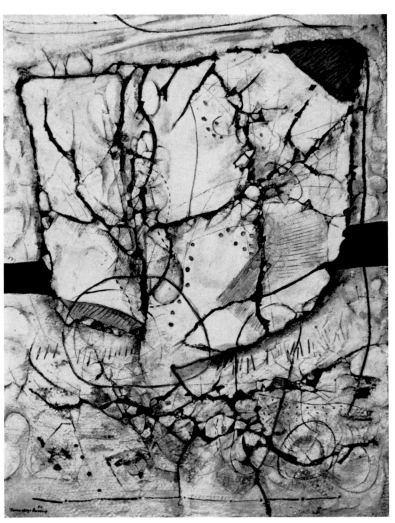

Tomoshige Kusuno. *What is the Plural Form of 'it'*? N.D.

Sergio Iberê Camargo. *Figure III* (*Figura III*). N.D.

Sergio Iberê Camargo. *Figure (Figura)*. 1964.

PRIMITIVE ART

The term 'primitive art' is a puzzling one, at least as it is applied to a certain contemporary mode. The works to which it refers often stand apart and cannot easily be evaluated by the same set of standards that serve, more or less, to define a sophisticated tradition.

Semantic confusion is part of the problem, since the connotations of the term are as diverse as they are blurred. Who and what is a 'primitive artist' today? Popularly – and inaccurately – someone who, living apart from the worldly currents of the age and unaware of them, finds refuge in an honest, naïve expression entirely of his own creation, and who therefore is free of external influences of any kind. Obviously, the artistic means employed by such a man cannot be traditional, since tradition is in itself collective and sophisticated rather than personal and naïve. The primitive painter according to such notions must be untaught yet able to resolve the complexities of pictorial language and its underlying techniques. For if he cannot, he is no artist – though primitive he may be. He is further, in the popular view, some sort of child who – despite age and experience, presumably through some process of artificial retardation – preserves an innocence that is, again falsely, equated with art or with the striving for pure expression. And, finally, he is often credited with possessing indigenous roots that his more sophisticated colleagues have, presumably, surrendered as a result of habitual imitation of international clichés.

None of this description makes sense, for art is neither unconscious, childlike, nor untaught. Nor is it viable outside a determining tradition. Least of all is it honest in a primitive sense. On the contrary, creative expression is artificial, devious, and dependent upon collective insights. This holds true even though the artist may be intuitively knowing rather than articulate, and even though he may have learned through empiric involvement with the materials of his craft rather than having been taught in an academy. Primitive art today then is primarily suspect. Closer investigation of specific works will almost certainly dissolve the contradiction in terms in the phrase 'primitive art' either by revealing those works as not so primitive or by stripping them of their claim to being art.

What may remain, after this kind of surgery, is so-called primitive art as a valid contemporary idiom. Latin American artists have availed themselves of such a pictorial language, occasionally with considerable success. Avoiding conventional solutions that today usually present themselves in the form of abstractly academic imitations, the so-called primitive artist is able to apply a skill with materials, often self-taught, to unfashionable subject-matter, thereby disguising considerable sophistication behind a naïve façade. Such methods (often employed by the artist with only half-awareness) when effective can result in a sort of double deception that beguiles the naïve viewer and delights the understanding participant. Our pleasurable reaction, in such instances, is legitimate, for art is never honest – in a primitive sense.

Raimundo de Oliveira. *Solomon and the Queen of Sheba (Salamão e a Rainha de Sabá)*. 1963.

RAIMUNDO DE OLIVEIRA

'God has created all things, God must be in all things.' Raimundo believes this and lives accordingly. His is a simple life, based on his love of painting and on his limited circle of close friends.

He was born and raised in Feira de Santana, State of Bahia, in the northeast of Brazil, where the African traditions of cult are intertwined with those of Brazilian Catholicism.

His devout mother wanted him to become a priest, and would let him read only the Bible and his school books. His father, who disapproved of his early efforts in painting, wanted his only son to become a respectable merchant, like himself.

There it began... the battle inside Raimundo that is still raging.

The Brazilian writer and critic Jorge Amado refers to Raimundo as a prophet. 'Through his hands,' writes Amado, 'he achieves the miracle of candor, peace, love, and joy, eliminating the violence of the Old Testament. This Raimundo is a prophet with the soul of St Francis of Assisi.'

Friends, however, also know of his unreachable inner solitude and of his intense struggle against unhappiness, which manifests itself sometimes in restlessness; since coming to São Paulo in 1958, Raimundo has moved more than fifty times. His good friend Júlio Pacello said, 'His normal state is unhappiness. That's why he paints happy pictures. He is a lonely man who is seldom alone... but we don't try to find perfection in our friends.'

Raimundo's greatest regret is that his father died before he could show him his success as a painter, a success which is considerable – all his paintings are sold before they are delivered to the galleries in São Paulo, Rio, Buenos Aires, and New York.

His mother, however, had been happy about her son's chosen work, and he remembers her words: 'Through painting the saints, my son is surely on his way to heaven.'

Raimundo lives now in his small apartment crammed with his in-progress paintings, all peopled with his funny angels with small wings and 'important personages' who 'must all have beards'. On his walls are collages made up of his mementoes of his mother, who died in 1953; of Carmen Miranda, whom he loved from afar; and of Pope John.

Raimundo loves his native Brazil, where people of many races live together amicably. Never would he want to live in a place 'where people do not like one another'. He is well known and loved in his neighborhood by the people he encounters in his daily round of life: the bartender José; Senhorinha Mercedes, the waitress in his 'regular' restaurant; his barber, Amérigo.

Twice he felt ready to enter a monastery, but his Catholicism was considered too unorthodox. 'I believe in God profoundly,' he said, 'and I believe that all religions lead to heaven. God is everywhere, including in the bar.

'The priests and the bishop thought I was crazy and had the devil in me. Today I am friendly with the Dominican fathers, who are very open. I take communion with them.'

Raimundo de Oliveira. *The Flagellation of Christ* (*La flagelação de Cristo*). 1964.

URUGUAY

Joaquín Torres García. *Construction with Primitive Forms (Constructivo con formas primitivas)*. 1932.

URUGUAYAN PAINTING

In terms of sheer numbers, I must have established some kind of a record during my breathless stay in Montevideo. My pace could not have been sustained at all, had it not been possible to dismiss many works out of hand, either because they were obviously inferior in quality or because they were clearly superficial and derivative.

Of artists visited, Ramos struck me most vividly as a painter of accomplishment and stature. In his studio, I raised the question of medium, since he appeared to be a draftsman rather than a painter. His reply was twofold: first, he pointed out that the fact that much of his work is executed in oil on paper would be sufficient to distinguish him from the draftsman. But, more important, he believed, like many contemporary artists, that rigid classification according to medium is no longer feasible at a time of material and technical proliferation. I would add that Ramos's black-and-white work on paper, despite its relatively small size, had more power and scope than most of the canvases I saw in Montevideo. His images, too, are convincing. Semi-abstract in nature, with a growing tendency toward explicit expressionism, they retain a very personal quality.

Ramos is singularly free from the tyranny, so powerful in Uruguay, of the great Torres García, many of whose works can be seen at the local museum. Torres García's distinct pictographic style and his restrained color range have impressed themselves upon his pupils and his pupils' pupils, but unhappily without transmitting the inner radiance that was his alone. This perhaps is as it must be and, all considered, is no worse than what happened to those who felt the direct influence of Mondrian, Kandinsky, or Jackson Pollock. Uruguay, however, is such a small country that the object lesson becomes painfully obvious.

Two painters who have made use of Torres García's legacy with a great degree of independence seem to me to be Ventayol and Gamarra. Among younger artists, Teresa Vila, who, like Ramos, also works in the graphic medium, seemed most promising. Her work still shows traces of her student phase, and it lacks the sure and authoritative stroke of her older colleagues. But her drawing is tender, subtle, and inventive, and has, in my judgment, an enviable potential for further growth.

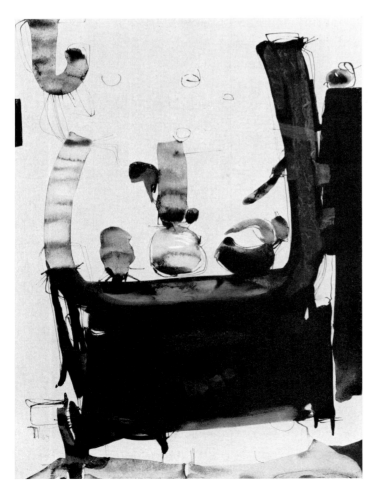

Teresa Vila. *¿Tomado...?* 1964.

Opposite: Nelson Ramos. *Couples between Bars* (*Hay parejas entre rejas*). 1964.

Nelson Ramos. *The Scream* (*El grito*). 1964.

ARGENTINA

José Antonio Fernández-Muro. *Secret Banner.* 1964.

Santiago
September 7, 1964

Mr Samuel Paz
Buenos Aires, Argentina

Dear Samuel:

During the four years since I last visited Buenos Aires, Argentine painting has changed markedly, and I found myself, as a result, confronting an almost entirely new scene. When I was in your city in 1960 there was a great deal of excitement over the emergence of a young group whose members were Fernández-Muro, Sarah Grilo, Clorindo Testa, Miguel Ocampo, and Kazuya Sakai. I chose one work by each artist to represent Argentina in the show at the Institute of Contemporary Art in Boston – the first contemporary Latin American selection, as far as I know, ever made by the director of a North American museum. The group, at any rate, is no longer in existence, although those who formed it continue to enjoy various degrees of success, mostly abroad. Only Testa among them continues to work in Buenos Aires, but only on a part-time basis, since he is so heavily committed to his successful architectural practice.

An important question, arising in connection with Latin American painters, and specifically with Argentina, concerns the uncommonly high rate of emigration among the best and most creative practitioners. Why is this so? Why do your painters feel compelled to go to New York, Paris, and Rome? Do they, by going abroad, resolve the problems that prompted their departure? Would you care to comment upon the effect of such mass movements on Buenos Aires as a center of the arts?

Upon acquainting myself with your current scene, I at first felt regret at so speedy an abdication by a group that I had come to regard highly. What is consoling, however, is that others have stepped into the breach so quickly – and in such astonishing numbers – to continue an active, fluid, and diverse tradition that was merely foreshadowed in previous generations.

Group formation, incidentally, seems to be the rule with you even if the ideological and stylistic basis for the group concept is tenuous. Through our own Guggenheim International Award Exhibition, held prior to my first visit this year, I became aware of your semi-figurative expressionists (Macció, Deira, de la Vega, and Noé), who, I am told, worked in one studio until recently, when half of the team deserted the front for positions behind the lines – Paris and New York. It is said they will be back, however, and so we shall see.

Then there are the local geometricians, also a foursome (Demarco, Mac-Entyre, Angel Vidal, and Tomasello), more uneven in quality than their expressionist counterparts and, despite a more demanding intellectual foundation, less sophisticated as painters.

The 'Phases' group in its Argentine reincarnation seems to me to be a highly brittle constellation in Buenos Aires despite the critic Julio Llinás's ability to breathe some substance into its abstract soul. Its artistic (as opposed to its literary) vitality depends upon paintings, not upon ideas, and the movement therefore sustains itself by dint of the good work of Peluffo and Polesello.

I would describe your groups at the moment – and probably only for the moment – as follows:

1. The generation, now middle-aged, of those painters who some five years ago were an active force in Buenos Aires;

2. The momentarily thinned ranks of contemporary expressionists, who, I believe, rightfully occupy the center of the stage;

3. The young geometricians, who when contrasted with the expressionists emphasize the multiplicity and breadth of your current scene;

4. The 'Phases' with its distinctly literary origins, depending upon isolated but notable contributors;

5. A particularly lively and diverse group of young talent, still in a blissful no-man's-land between play and work, whose creations range from advertising Pop to popular Argentine myth, from hearts and white flowers to graveyard humor and death masks, from painted mattresses to sculpture stepping out of flat canvases. Not all of their works are equally valid or equally silly. It will be interesting and probably a little sad to watch this young talent grow up.

6. The important formations abroad, particularly the Argentine members of the Recherche d'Art Visuel in Paris. They made a strong showing at the Nouvelle Tendance show at the Musée des Arts Décoratifs in 1964 and are, of course, of particular interest to the friends of Op.

With all of this group talk, one must not forget the individual, nonaligned painters, of whom there are a few good ones and who in this somewhat overorganized milieu might be said to resemble a group of lone wolves. Nor should one forget that some good sculptors serve as exceptions to an otherwise conspicuous dearth in sculptural attainment that exists almost uniformly throughout Latin America.

There is, of course, no doubt about Argentina's pre-eminence in the art of painting among the republics of Latin America today.

Kind regards,
T. M. M.

Kazuya Sakai. *Painting (Pintura)*. 1963.   Sarah Grilo. *Untitled*. 1964.

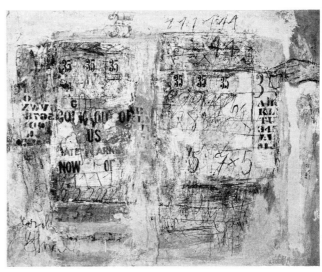

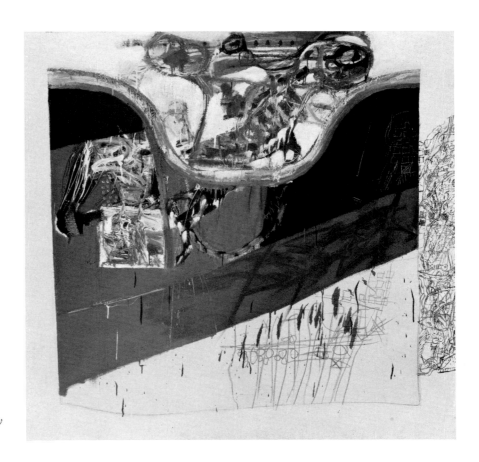

Rómulo Macció. *The President on the Balcony*
(*El presidente en el balcón*). 1963.

Rómulo Macció. *That Crazy Brother of Theo*
(*Aquel hermano loco de Theo*). N.D.

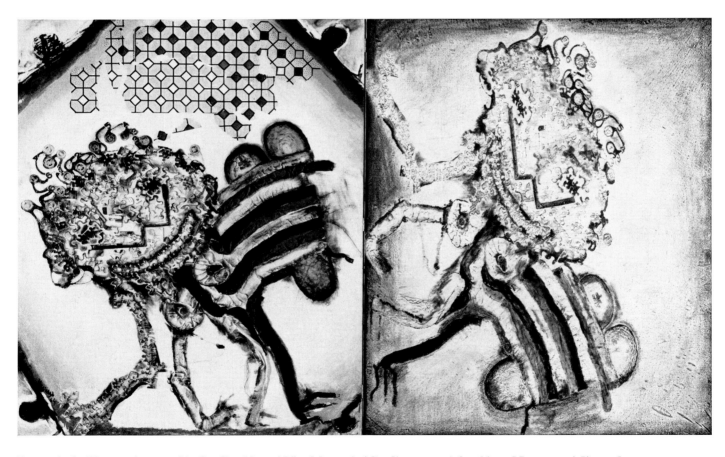

Opposite top: Ernesto Deira. *Around Thought 'A' (No. 4) (En torno al pensamiento 'A' [No. 4]).* 1964.

Bottom: Jorge de la Vega. *Anamorphic Conflict No. 1 (The Measurement) (Conflicto anamórfico No. 1 [La medida]).* 1964.

Jorge de la Vega. *Anamorphic Conflict No. 3 (The Memory) (Conflicto anamórfico No. 3 [La memoria]).* 1964.

Buenos Aires
May 3, 1965

Dear Tom:

A lot of water has gone under the bridge in the four years between your visits here. Every year has seen new generations of painters, each with its young men whose drive for experimentation gives life to their work and sparks a fresh wave of public interest. This characteristic is the determining factor of change in the Buenos Aires art world. I mention the city specifically because it is here that all Argentine art activity is centered.

What you say is true. When our artists reach a certain level, a certain stage in their career, they feel a need to experience life away from Buenos Aires. There are many reasons for this. In the first place, the crisis in Argentina and the permanency which that crisis is acquiring impel one, artist or no, to seek his own solutions, to look for better conditions abroad. Then, too, quite a few foreign art critics have come here in the past three years and have stimulated those among our artists who are beginning to achieve international recognition. There is also the need to visit the fountainheads of painting past and present; bear in mind that the cubist paintings of Picasso and the work of Mondrian have never been seen here except in reproduction.

Finally, there is the desire to measure oneself against those who have achieved success. This is often the most valid reason... and the most cruel. It is a reversal of the pattern followed by the preceding generations, who used to 'study' in Rome or Paris and return to make a place for themselves, to be consecrated 'maestros'.

Quite a few Argentine artists have established themselves abroad. Among them one must single out members of the Groupe de Recherche d'Art Visuel de Paris or of the École de Paris, such as Alicia Peñalba, Sergio de Castro, and other long-time residents of France. There are also some Argentine painters in Rome. Ulm has attracted some artists and theoreticians who were part of the 'Solid' movement in the Buenos Aires of 1950. For some years, New York has also welcomed a few Argentine painters. That city has become a Mecca for young men who want to travel. I believe that soon you will be having our artists as regular visitors, not only in such places as the Walker Art Center of Minneapolis, which recently exhibited the 'New Art of Argentina' selection, but in other cities as well.

The Argentine artist knows a great deal. He knows how to make a living. He has a great knack for finding the right place to settle in an unknown city and for making the most of his situation. Yet, for all this, the Argentine seldom takes root in foreign soil; for all his complaints about the problems besetting his country, his deep feeling of nostalgia eventually forces him to return home.

Travels and long stays in foreign countries serve to siphon off enough art to prevent the flooding of our limited market. But they also present the possibility of serious conflict. When some of our traveling artists return to take up permanent residence in Buenos Aires, they will find that the scene has undergone considerable change and that their places have been taken by others. Rather than risk this eventuality, some artists limit the length of their trips abroad so as not to undermine their position at home. Naturally, this sort of maneuver does not allow them to gain an outstanding position in the international art world.

Antonio Seguí. *After that Misfortune*
(*Después de aquella desgracia*). 1964.

Antonio Seguí. *Portrait of a Friend*
(*Retrato de un amigo*). 1964.

I agree with you that the speed with which artists are recognized is surprising. Doubtless, many factors play a part. The principal one is that though we have advanced far, we cannot yet clearly discern an upward movement in the careers of our young painters and sculptors. They are strongly endowed from the beginning. They seem to acquire a high level of proficiency relatively soon. But this initial attainment is not followed by sufficient self-analysis, by an introspection that would allow them to develop what they have begun in such promising fashion.

To comment on your observations about our groups, you must not assume that groups are the rule. To make that assumption would be to give them too formal a meaning, a connotation of program making, and this is not usually the case. More often than not, forming a group is simply a way to open fire and fight the first battle. There is little cohesion among members. Of the Deira–de la Vega–Macció–Noé group, Macció has been away from Buenos Aires for a year, Noé has just returned after a year in New York, and the others have made shorter trips. In most cases, the formation of a group adds nothing to the values of the individual members and detracts nothing from their individual independence.

Something similar can be said of the Mac-Entyre–Brizzi–Vidal–Silva group whom you describe as our 'ideal geometricians'. They are called a group only because of the need for some term to distinguish between generations. Although these people are not lineal descendants of the 'solid' movement of the fifties, they do represent a spirit of plastic order that appears to have endured these last two decades. Demarco and Tomasello, who are now living in Paris, are totally independent of them.

The 'Phases' group developed a clear and outspoken position about life, a position carried to high levels in literature by Julio Llinás. He was the lodestone for the plasticists – for Martha Peluffo (his wife); for Rogelio Polesello, now apparently an independent; for Borda, who has returned after a scholarship in Paris; and for Chab, who has had two shows at the Organization of American States in Washington. I believe the group has lost much of its charm and that its members have realized or will soon realize that the spirit that gave life to 'Phases' has evaporated.

Another group you refer to in your letter – Sarah Grilo, Fernández-Muro, Miguel Ocampo, Kazuya Sakai, and Clorindo Testa – emerged after their exhibition in 1960 at the Museo Nacional de Bellas Artes in Buenos Aires. These people represented a cornerstone of the new painting. Yet two years later, the group all but dissolved.

This review would not be complete without mention of the newer artists, some of whom may be full of surprises: Marta Minujín, Emilio Renart, Delia Puzzovio. On the periphery are the solitary painters, Aizenberg and Magariños D.

I do not expect too much to evolve out of the present situation in sculpture. Badii and Iommi are still working, but among the young sculptors there is no one who in my judgment is outstanding.

Still, it is not being too optimistic to suppose that something important can result from all this effervescence.

Sincerely,
Samuel Paz

Luis Felipe Noé. *When the Sun Warms the Homeland*
(*Cuando calienta el sol en la patria*). 1963.

Luis Felipe Noé. *Fire at the Jockey Club*. 1963.

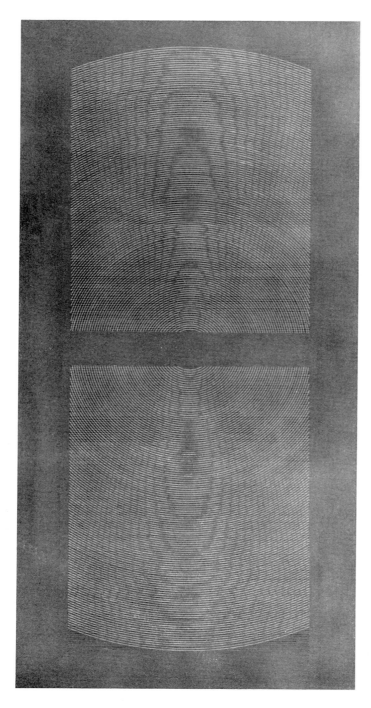

Eduardo Mac-Entyre. *Generative Painting. Weave No. 4*
(*Pintura generativa. Trama No. 4*). 1964.

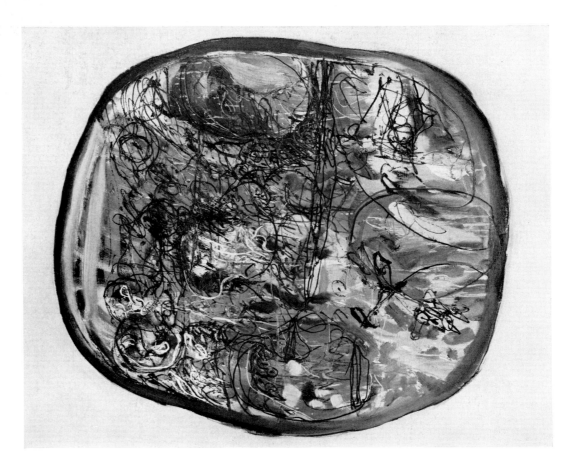

Ernesto Deira. *Simple Remembrance (Recuerdo simple)*. 1964.

Nicolás García Uriburu. *Paraná River (Río Paraná)*. 1964.

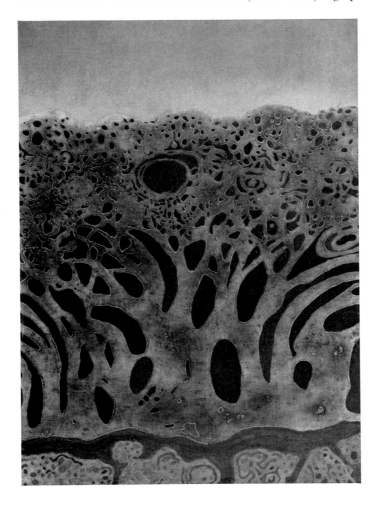

Marta Minujín. *Foot (Pie)*. N.D.

Pablo Roberto Suarez. *Crazy Baby (Muñeca brava)*. 1964.

Honorio Morales. *Positive (Positivo)*. 1964.

Delia Puzzovio. *Wreath for Inhuman Inhabitants*. 1964.

Victor Magariños D. *Painting (Pintura)*. 1963.

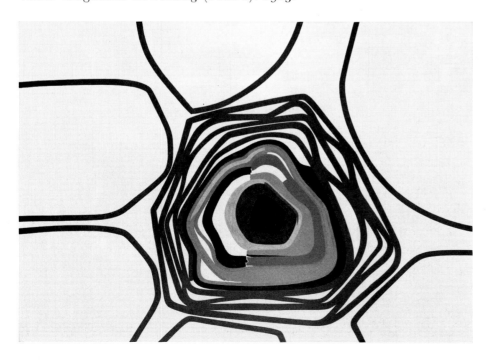

ROGELIO POLESELLO

The address is 2101 Federico Lacroze – a large house with an air of decaying elegance in a tree-shaded residential district of Buenos Aires.

In the front yard lies 'Valentine', an almost human dummy with a broken arm, the gift of a sculptor that somehow serves as a warning to the unwary visitor of the small world inside, which is always lively and sometimes rather frantic. Here are the studios of Martha Peluffo and Rogelio Polesello, and here live Vittorio Minardi, a philosopher and translator who specializes in Marx and Hegel; the poet Balducci; the ex-priest, now painter, Iramain; the former painter, now dancer, Gioia Fiorentino; another painter, Mapaey; the actor and film maker Albeac; and the doctor Mendes. Also here is María Helena, once the maid of an artist who lived in the house. He left; she liked the place so well she stayed.

'The confrontation of this kind of life', says Martha, 'has helped us all. What matters with us, those who live in the house and those with whom we regularly meet – the one central thing that unites us – is the need to experience the world.

'The house was born shortly after I was married,' recalls Martha. She and her husband, the poet and critic Julio Llinás, lost their studio and had to find a new place to work. The house seemed to have many virtues – a major one being that though the ceilings were high, the rent was low. 'Some rooms were large and some were small, but they all had one thing in common: they were in miserable condition. With three other painters, including Polesello, we rented the place.

'Julio was the intellectual motor of the house,' Martha continued. 'He took a definite position toward painting. We formed a group called "Phases". Our attitude favored lyrical abstraction, taking into account some aspects of surrealism.

'At first the group centered around Julio, but then, as is usual in groups, everyone took his own road. In the beginning we were all painters, but the house kept on changing until today's mixture was achieved.

'Julio introduced us to the surrealist poets,' Martha said. 'Vittorio told us of Marx and Hegel.

MARTHA PELUFFO

Other poets and writers congregate here at night. It does not matter what your politics are or what social class you come from. We talk and drink and paint incessantly. There are many strong points of contact, but there is privacy too. For example, I know what Vittorio thinks about philosophy and politics, but I know almost nothing about his family.

'On the other hand, Gioia's mother comes and raises hell in the garden about her way of life. There is only one phone in the house and we hear all the conversations. We need not eavesdrop; Gioia comes and tells us all about it. She terrorizes us with her radical changes of professions and boy friends.'

Martha says she became a painter because 'I was shy and had to express myself. A white canvas is a beautiful thing. One never knows what it will become'.

Painting for Martha is a happy thing, and Julio describes her as 'the ardent eye'.

Rogelio Polesello, a bachelor, was the only one who lived in the house in the early days. The others came only to work. 'I had a battle with my father and I came with my valise and bed,' Rogelio recalls. 'The house seemed to have ghosts then. I worked until 3 A.M. most nights and would hear all sorts of creaking noises. One night the gate collapsed.

'During the first year we were working together and separately and we had our first joint show.... The best years of my life have passed in this house. It has a beautiful terrace, and under it pass the most beautiful girls, and some of them enter.'

And then there is the view of the nonpainter. The philosopher Vittorio says: 'There is no water and there are rats. When it rains, it rains in, and all these faults make me live happily with contradictions.

'Humanly, there is great rapport among those who live here. What interests me tremendously,' he adds with a trace of jealousy, 'is how quickly these painters can finish a canvas.'

Aldo Pellegrini, a noted critic and frequent visitor, has paid a tribute to the house by comparing it to the famous Montmartre atelier where Renoir, Picasso, and Modigliani worked. 'This house,' he said, 'is the "Bateau Lavoir" of Argentine painting.'

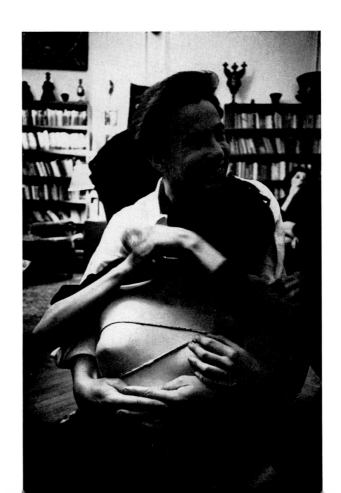

Martha Peluffo. *Blind Island* (*Isla ciega*). 1964.

Rogelio Polesello. *Kaleidoscope (Caleidoscopio)*. 1964.

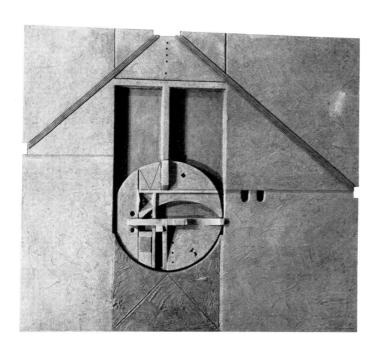

Marcelo Bonevardi. *Astrolabio*. 1964.

Marcelo Bonevardi. *The Architect*. 1964.

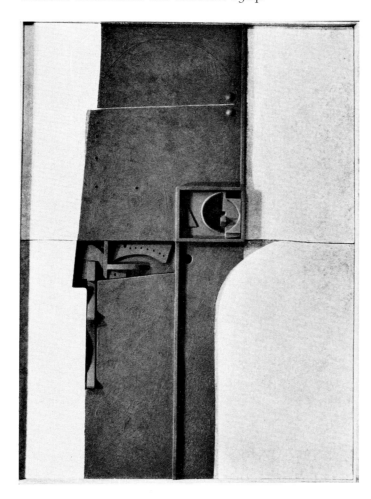

EXPATRIATES: NEW YORK

Hundreds of Latin American painters have found a home, temporary or permanent, in New York: Fernández-Muro, Sarah Grilo, Sakai, Noé, and Bonevardi from Argentina; Nemesio Antúnez, Castrocid, and Nuñez from Chile; María Pacheco from Bolivia; Armando Morales from Nicaragua; Botero from Colombia, and a host of others. Some have made notable inroads upon the rather rigidly defined New York hierarchies by gaining representation in top galleries and in distinguished private and public collections.

The exhibition called 'Magnet', organized by the Inter-American Foundation for the Arts at the Galería Bonino in the fall of 1964, served as a progress report of work accomplished by New York City's Latin American contingent.

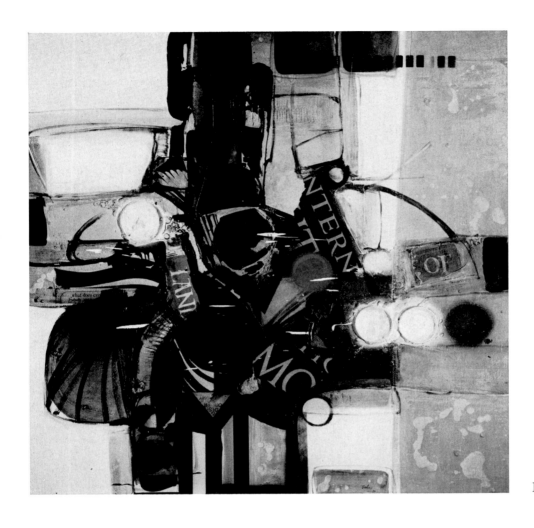

Kazuya Sakai. *The Bridge*. 1964.

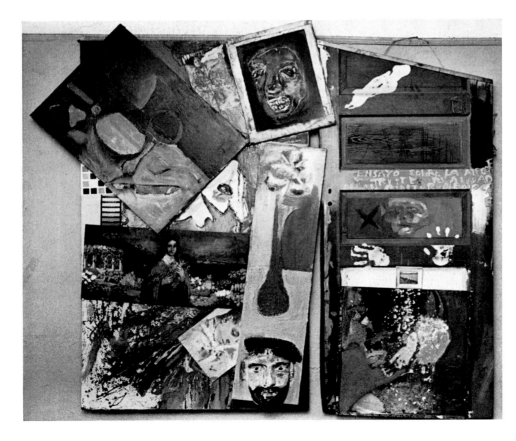

Sarah Grilo. *Inferno (Infierno)*. 1964.

Opposite: Luis Felipe Noé. *Treatise on the Gay and Sad Reality of a Mediocre Artist (Ensayo sobre la alegre y triste realidad de un pintor mediocre)*. N.D.

JOSÉ ANTONIO FERNÁNDEZ-MURO

The lives of Spanish-born Argentinean José Antonio Fernández-Muro and his painter-wife Sarah Grilo flow in a New York pattern: 'You work all day,' says Fernández-Muro, 'and three or four evenings a week you go to shows, openings, or parties. On Tuesdays, there are openings in the galleries, two or three that night. You go to the A.F.A., to Bonino's, to Marlborough. You meet artists of all nationalities, many from Latin America, dealers, collectors, friends.... You end up having a meal at the Gaucho Restaurant in the Village.... Often you are tired... but you go all the same.... It is one way of meeting and talking to people.... After late nights the mornings are difficult.... It is all very exhausting, but by noon we are usually at work.'

'New York', Fernández-Muro says, 'is where all artistic directions and movements converge. They all mingle, cook, and boil, and out of the mixture emerges the most important ambience of international artistic life. This climate also has its disadvantages, however. Here the public seems to expect the sensational and the spectacular and to embrace newness for its own sake. It is conditioned to desire the latest thing without giving thought to its true value. Such an attitude can lead to a medium of expression that is both frivolous and superficial.

'The artist works in a decadent society, for a decadent society. The people he wants to get across to are often either uninterested or simply nonexistent. There are more museums and galleries, more interest in culture than ever before, but the artist continues to be as isolated and as lonely as he has always been.'

Why did the Fernández-Muros decide to make their home in New York? 'For me,' says Fernández-Muro, 'New York is *the* Big City. One either lives there or in a fishing village in Spain. Either may be horrible to stay in all the time unless you can somehow offset one with the other.... In Argentina there are many difficulties in life and work, many unimportant but annoying things that make concentration quite impossible. Since we felt that nothing we could do would influence or change anything there we thought we must leave.'

The Fernández-Muros have a full family life. Their son Juan Antonio goes to high school; their young married daughter Verónica has presented them with Caroline, an enchantress now four months old. When Caroline comes with her parents to visit, all painting stops. Sarah and Antonio coo as all grandparents do.

How did New York affect Fernández-Muro's work? 'When I came to New York I saw manhole covers in the streets and their shape and beauty struck me. I incorporated them in my paintings not for their anecdotal or documentary effect but because they were similar to the forms that I used before in my geometric paintings.'

New York has many beautiful manhole covers. When Fernández-Muro tires of them, there will always be the Spanish village. 'Once one leaves one's own country, one becomes a nomad,' he says. 'Keep on returning home but always leave again... to have another experience.'

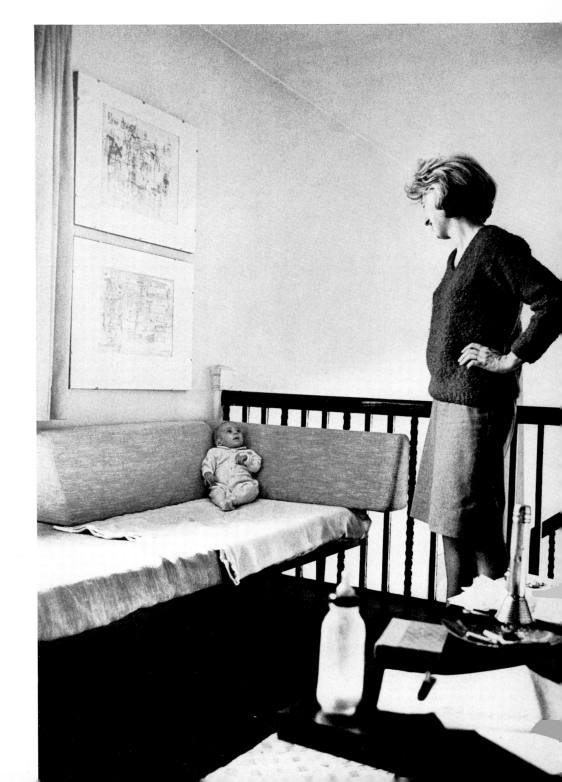

José Antonio Fernández-Muro. *To the Great People of Argentina (Al gran pueblo argentino)*. 1964.

CHILE

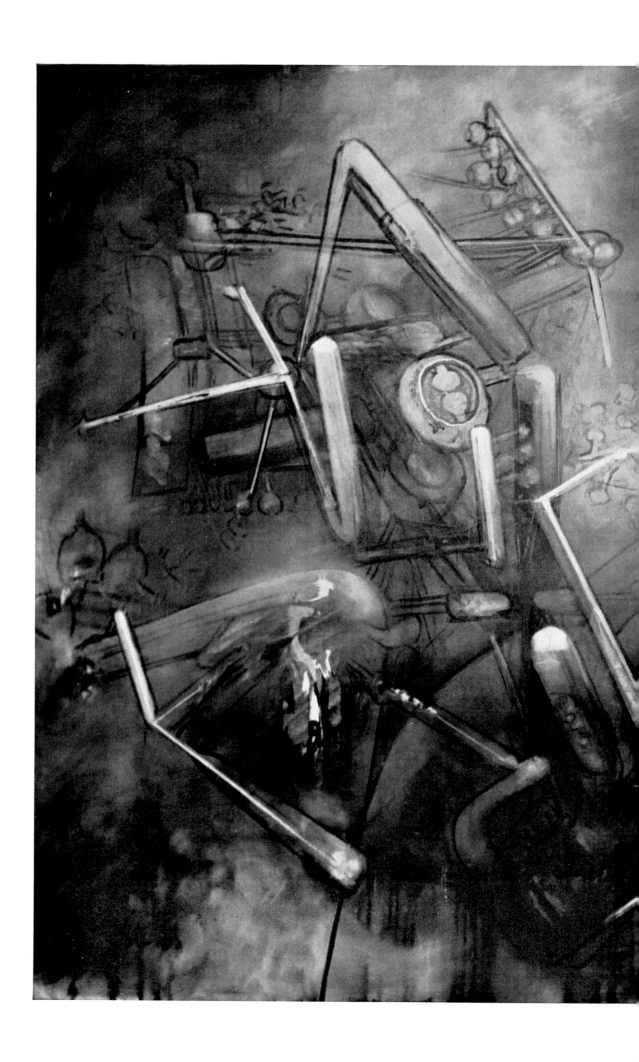

Matta (Roberto Sebastián Antonio Matta Echaurren). *Untitled*. 1962–1963.

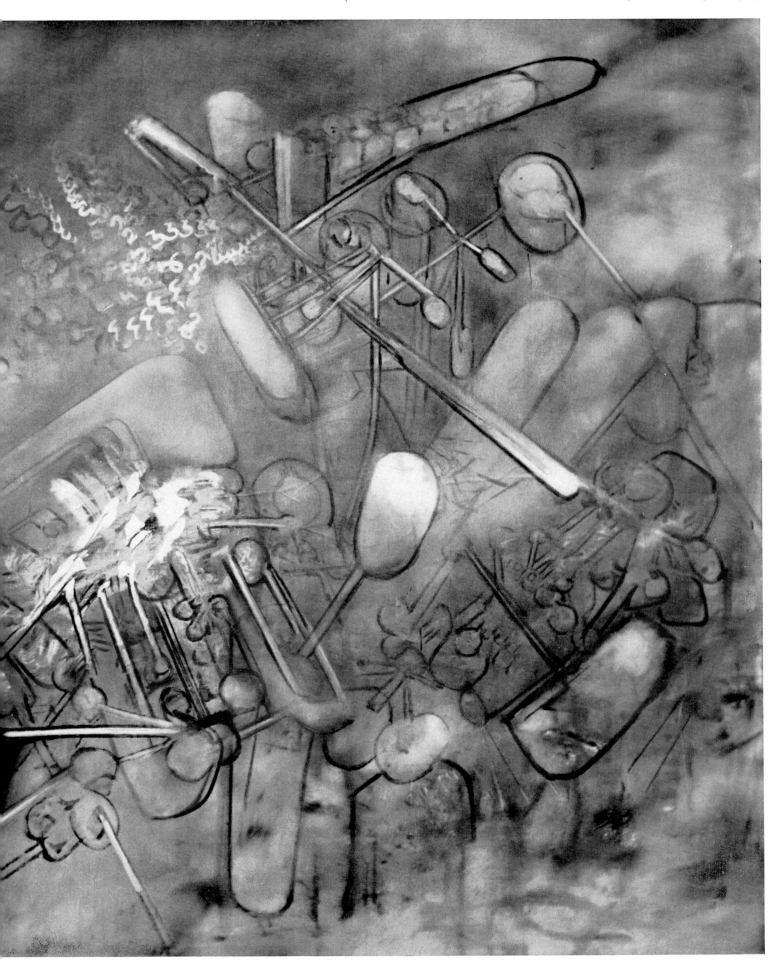

RICARDO YRARRÁZAVAL

'I am a slow painter.'

The voice is deliberate yet dreamy; smoke wafts, and Yrarrázaval's eyes become reflective and his mind seems to turn inward. He recalls a trip to the altiplano of Peru and Bolivia some years ago: 'I stopped painting completely for three years after that trip.... It's only now that some of those colors are coming back.'

The small and secluded house of Yrarrázaval is a happy anomaly. It is a portion of Montparnasse transported to Santiago. Here he lives an intense artist's life in the framework of a closely knit family.

Yrarrázaval is ruggedly built and likes the outdoors but shuts all the daylight out of his attic studio. He paints with deep, brooding concentration and explosive action, approaching his canvas like a bullfighter the bull, full of mistrust, carefully watching every detail, lunging at it with sudden thrusts. He must not be distracted. The stairs to his studio lead to a locked door, without a knob, and the children know the rule.

'When Ricardo works, we don't see anyone for weeks on end. We don't go out of the house,' says his wife, Isabel, with a shy and charming smile, voicing a fact, without a trace of discontent.

She also has a key to the studio and slips in quietly. If Ricardo asks her to look she does, and their heads incline together. Otherwise she withdraws to the corner couch and knits in silence.

She understands the importance of the unconscious presence of those he loves but who must not interfere. They are his roots; without them there is no bloom.

Isabel and Ricardo met and married in Paris ten years ago. She had grown up in his section of Santiago and he had known her as a child, but he had not seen her for many years. Like the colors of the altiplano, this came back too.

Yrarrázaval is shy but has ambition. He knows that maturity takes time and he is old fashioned enough to want it to come naturally, through work.

His needs are simple, and one feels that in his house is his world entire.

Ricardo Yrarrázaval. *Ancestral Presence (Presencia ancestral)*. 1964.

Ricardo Yrarrázaval. *Face (Rostro)*. 1964.

Lima
September 10, 1964

Mr Jorge Elliott
Santiago, Chile

Dear Jorge:

In general, in the three days I spent in Santiago I found less satisfaction with the present state than perhaps some hope for the future. With very few exceptions your painters seemed to have arrived at a level of attainment that we have come to associate with regional accomplishments in the United States. Like our best regional painters, your artists command considerable skill of execution within areas well traveled by others. Their models are often obvious – Matta, Dubuffet, de Staël – to mention the most recurrent ones. At other times a combination of influences can be traced that are usually not fused into a statement of sufficient clarity to stand on its own or to command attention.

In our conversations you formulated the distinction between the creative and the interpretative arts – a distinction usually applied to music or the theater, where characteristically the creator and interpreter have separate functions. The composer and the pianist, the playwright and the actor, with such intermediary agents as the conductor and the producer, exemplify the distinction. Painters, on the other hand, are technically speaking always creators (since there is no intermediary between the inventive act and its execution). Your point, however, was that by producing variations on a well-known theme, the craftsman without a clearly identifiable creative personality becomes in fact the executor of commonly held plastic ideas, i.e. an interpreter. The point is, I think, well taken, and I believe it is applicable to most of your good artists.

Among those who transcend this definition, it seems to me, is Ricardo Yrarrázaval – a very fine painter indeed. Clearly the interpretative limitation does not apply to him, for his statements – few as they are – are highly authoritative and by now largely independent of such models as he followed a few years ago. My visit to his studio was revealing, even though he could show me only two of his recently finished works, one of which displeased him. What interested me was his earlier work of the fifties, when, as interpreter himself, he was playing variations on themes by de Staël. From the early sixties on, quite possibly aided by his experience as a ceramist, he seemed to come into his own with form-and-color solutions clearly announcing his current stage. Yet precisely at this point Yrarrázaval stopped painting for three years, as he told me, to gather himself and to rethink his work as a painter. He then resumed, without a break in continuity, and asserted his newly found maturity. His work is abstract, although the feminine form (which he explores almost obsessively as a draftsman) seems to underlie his images. One cannot miss the pre-Columbian, indigenous connotations. These are evoked in part by the shapes that distantly relate to ceramic forms but more through the glowing, sun-parched colors that make up his palette and enliven his surfaces. It would be difficult to imagine such painting originating in Paris or New York. Yrarrázaval is visibly but unself-consciously Latin American, and he achieves this identity without pictorialism, through purely formal means and from within.

Among painters previously unknown to me there were a few who seemed to do serious and dedicated work. Balmes, Nuñez, and two or three others seem to be finding themselves in their most recent work. A few years, no doubt, will provide answers regarding their further development.

Some of your painters draw very well, and as in other parts of Latin America there is lively graphic activity. Unfortunately it often infringes upon painting instead of aiding it as one assumes it should. Rosa Vicuña, I think, is a fine sculptress, and the isolated examples of sculpture that I saw by youngsters make me think that this medium bears watching in Chile. And, of course, there are the primitives and quasi-primitives, who always provide special problems of evaluation.

Chile is one of the most beautiful countries in the world. Your mountain ranges running parallel to the seacoast are spectacular beyond words – and apparently beyond evocation, for your painters seem to withdraw into an inner landscape that perhaps has a good deal of meaning for them and, in any case, avoids a confrontation with that overwhelming scenery that may be hard to sustain. I am sure that in this predicament your painters' prudence is well advised, but I would not mind seeing some evidence that the visual raw material has been confronted.

Best regards,
T. M. M.

Guillermo Nuñez. *Freedom is our Business.* 1965.

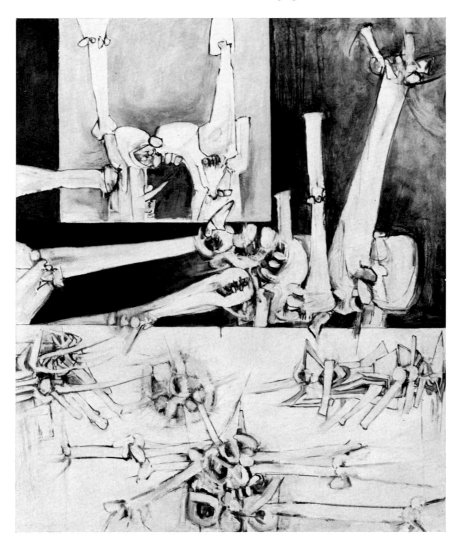

Dear Tom:

I am glad you remember our talk on the possibility of most serious artists being creative interpreters rather than inventive creators. Dissatisfaction with the way the plastic arts are being appraised at present has led me to question quite a number of accepted aesthetic beliefs in the light of my own experience as an artist.

The problem of creativity was one of the first to come to my notice. One aspect of it – perhaps the least subjective – interested me particularly, because I felt that as it is generally seen it hampers criticism considerably. I refer to the question of interpreters vs. authentic creators. I soon realized that it was not enough to call the intermediaries interpreters in those arts that need intermediaries between the creative act and its execution. In that case, arts such as painting which do not need them could only be seen exclusively as arts of pure creation. At any moment the critics could begin to demand absolute creativity from anyone wielding a brush for expressive purposes. I later found that there were any number of interesting composers – men like César Franck whose work is not academic – who had labored with materials invented by others and whose absolute creativity was very much inferior to that of composers like Stravinsky, for example. On the other hand, I also grew to feel that interpreters such as Arrau or Toscanini were quite as creative as any significant minor composer. I then had to ask myself to what extent a painter such as Sisley was a creative interpreter and not an authentic inventive creator. Surely a vast number of significant painters were executors, with individual variations, of commonly held plastic ideas. Furthermore, there is bound to be a measure of interpretative creative ability in all people of judgment, insight, and feeling for art, including critics. Perhaps, then, when circumstances weaken an art, insight and creativity in the critic's mind lose their balance until the critic is quite liable to project more significance onto the art he examines than is warranted. Indeed, he can come to use insignificant art as a starting point for a creation of his own, while demanding excessive creative ability from everyone and overlooking potent interpretative variations. I fear that this happens all too frequently today.

Therefore, I cannot fully agree with you when you conclude that my flimsy theory holds true for the regional artists of the United States but not for the artist who happens to succeed in New York. I will not deny that there are perhaps five or six authentic creators in that city, but in all likelihood most of the reputed artists there are in reality spurious inventors. In large urban centers one is more likely to acquire polish and *savoir faire*, a sophistication that in an artist can be deceptive, especially when experimentation is much in demand and critics' judgments have little to fall back on.

Provincialism – and you, with certain justification, deem most Chilean art to be provincial – was not always a synonym for awkwardness and derivative inexpressiveness. When one examines two pots, one from Mochica and another from Nazca, one is impressed by their beauty and sophisticated formal fitness; and yet they were made by craftsmen belonging to small river-valley cultures separated by vast tracts of desert, utterly out of touch with one another and most of the world, at least in the sense that we, today, are all in touch. The same can be said for the art one finds in many old small

European towns that once flourished in splendid isolation. The limitations of provincialism today are the consequence not of a lack but of an excess of communications. Provincial art is generally executed by thoroughly informed people who mistrust their own environment, people for whom culture is always *elsewhere*. Yet if culture is not among people it is nowhere. Culture today is seen as an elusive quality which suddenly fixes itself on one or another major urban center, from which it has to be imported. I rather think that it is more like a magnetic field that grows about a conductor as it transmits electricity.

The strong image most rich nations project, mainly through their large urban centers, on smaller nations and on distant regions of their territory interferes with the local image of life, so that artists in small countries and in the provinces tend not to live their reality, tend not to function in terms of their genuine experience, and are therefore weakened in their expressiveness. But, at the same time, all educated humanity today surely lives life, as sheer life, less and less, and intellectualizes it more and more. We have all become excessively self-conscious and idea-conscious. We move along, ruminating enormous quantities of information, hardly aware of life itself. Artists in large urban centers are just as affected by this situation as are provincial artists, and if they do not have to carry the load of external cultural images to the same extent, they are, on the other hand, constantly pressed by all sorts of equivocal forces to perform the most appalling contortions imaginable. Critical future-directedness plays into the hands of present-day commercialism, which caters to our insatiable thirst for novelties. The plastic arts are particularly vulnerable to commercial exploitation because they always produce objects that can be marketed and can be owned more exclusively than any expensive car. But to increase the novelty value of cars, new models have to be designed every year, whether they are needed or not. One is certainly justified in one's belief that frequently new movements in art are promoted in every metropolis of the world today for similar reasons. In the meantime academism is not being avoided. A spurious invention can be as empty a husk as any picture hung during the nineteenth century in the Royal Academy.

I do not think that a distinction between provincialism and sophisticated urbanism can be considered as a transcendent issue. The faults of one are obvious and naïve, but the faults of the other may be more vicious and the virtues merely illusory. If there is any issue it probably involves authenticity of experience or something of the kind. Take the art of children, for example. Never academic, it has been the same everywhere through the ages and always seems fresh. It is original because its origin is so humanly pristine, and yet newness is of no account when we come to see it. Is newness really so important? Lawrence Alloway is fond of quoting Baudelaire's remark in his *The Painter of Modern Life*: 'Modernity is that which is ephemeral, fugitive, contingent upon the occasion.' But perhaps there is an occasion that persists through the ages. We continue to feel the fascination of Negro and pre-Columbian art, while we clutter museums of modern art with objects considered ephemeral, fugitive, contingent upon the occasion. There is a contradiction somewhere! I would not maintain that some apparently ephemeral art, contingent upon the occasion, cannot arise at moments of bewilderment and revulsion, but if it does it should not replace but coexist with one that is less circumstantial. I wonder whether this possibility is sufficiently kept in mind today.

You talk of the prudence of Chilean painters. Chileans are indeed a cautious people.

Chile's political history, especially of late, gives proof of that. Yet Chile changes surprisingly. So does Chilean painting, and you are right in believing that it is worth watching. I would be the last to assert that Chilean painting now constitutes a new and original formulation. What brings about an original national artistic formulation is a mystery into which I will not delve here. In Chile it has only happened in the field of poetry. At a given moment the language, and surely something beyond it, allowed poets such as Huidobro, Neruda, Gabriela Mistral, Díaz Casanueva, Nicanor Parra, Enrique Lihn, and several others to find their true voice. I doubt whether poetry in the United States is as significant as modern Chilean poetry. Nothing equivalent really has happened in the plastic arts.

But there are some healthy indications. We have, for instance, exported Matta, to whom American painting owes a great deal. Nemesio Antúnez's imagery is very much his own; I would not call his work provincial. If I have any quarrel with it, it is that I find it unpainterly, as I do most of the works of painters who, like Antúnez, were trained as architects – including Matta. Whether this really matters I do not know. On the other hand, the work of Ricardo Yrarrázaval, which you so much admire, is definitely painterly. He is one of the significant manifestations of possible improvement in a Chilean plastic idiom. Figures underlie his abstraction, simplified into elementary forms earthy as Chimu pots, or striped like Indian textiles; but the surprising thing is that he does not lose his refinement, his painter's instinct, and because he is not *trying* to be Latin American – there is no one less intellectual than Yrarrázaval – he is simply doing his best to paint well, and the images he sets down impose themselves on him unself-consciously. No. There is no reason to be pessimistic. You, in the short time that you were in Chile, came across two authentic creators, Rosa Vicuña and Yrarrázaval, which is not bad.

José Balmes. *Peace (Paz)*. 1964.

Of the relatively few sculptors in Chile, quite a number are very promising. I agree with your opinion of Rosa Vicuña's work. She is another potter at heart, fond of the red clay of our America. Her formal inventions, though abstract, have an organic vitality, and her wonderful objects, tenderly modeled, are alive, even endowed with a curious sexuality.

I have always held that we live in an age of artists rather than of art. I doubt very much whether we can talk of a really valid and convincing formulation in painting as existing anywhere. The future may judge our time as expressive, even unusually so. Yet I feel certain very few pockets of consistently potent artistry will be found contributing to the situation, but rather a scattering of individual geniuses over the face of the earth. Most of them, of course, have fertilized the ground about them for a short while, never for very long.

Perhaps we should forget beauty and even significant form and start thinking about art in terms of *knowledge*. When we come in touch with the art of primitive peoples we are before their whole knowledge. Their art gave them knowledge, concrete form, or it aimed at neutralizing those powers they considered menacing. Since rational man has delegated the function of seeking knowledge to science, art has been taken to be a kind of activity aimed at capturing abstract aesthetic qualities, which can all too easily become conventions, mannerisms, the beginnings of academism. No wonder Gauguin spoke of man recapturing his savagery. But by that I do not understand a return to the native, but rather a capacity for direct living. Artists must cease to be self-conscious, must unclutter their minds, and certainly, most certainly, they must never follow fashions. Perhaps the fact that Chilean art is slightly out of fashion has a little to do with your judging it as provincial... but what a good thing that it is!

Best regards,
Jorge Elliott

PERU

Mr Carlos Rodríguez Saavedra
Lima, Peru

Dear Carlos Rodríguez:

My stay in Peru was not very long, but I doubt that my impressions would have changed a great deal even if I could have stayed a fortnight. You have, it seems to me, an ensemble of painters counting among their numbers some skillful performers but only one soloist of exceptional capacity.

I am referring to Fernando de Szyszlo, a painter of true stature, who, together with a handful of equally gifted practitioners in other Latin American republics, carries your continental standard. Szyszlo is one of the few painters with whom a Latin American quality is an attribute of form rather than a pictorial reference. He is inevitably Peruvian as Braque is inevitably French in his work, although he is bound to share the universal concerns and awarenesses that all artists today have in common.

What seems most important to me in Szyszlo's work is the intensive presence of content with definable visual, literary, and formal components. The visual element comes to the fore in Szyszlo's landscape allusions, which at times are traceable to a particular reminiscence of the Peruvian landscape. The literary component, always present in cultivated minds, tends, in Szyszlo's case, to focus upon indigenous themes, which then strengthen the native timbre already contained in the visual allusion. Finally, the formal component, evolving from cubism and deriving its initial momentum from Tamayo, furnishes the channel through which visual and literary allusions can be brought to the surface.

As with Tamayo, or for that matter with Obregón of Colombia and Yrarrázaval of Chile, the distinction between figurative and nonfigurative art, which concerns the public so much, is without meaning, for neither category is strictly applicable. Szyszlo's is not an art that can be separated from the palpable reality of the observed world, nor does it imitate such reality. Rather, it would seem, are we viewing formal analogies, parables if you wish, whose ideated transformations read like distant memories of the observed. From this act of mutation comes the evocative power of Szyszlo's forms, which contain a reality substance far exceeding in meaningfulness the observed fact or the literary plot from which they ultimately derive.

To some degree this process is, of course, inherent in artistic creation in general and therefore not a particular feature of Szyszlo's painting. It is rare, however, to see the uniquely personal and the generally valid, the indigenous motivation and the international common denominator, so intensively interlocked; nor among your contemporary painters are imagery and form as readily identifiable and yet fused into a coherent statement as is the case with Szyszlo.

With kind regards,

Sincerely,
T. M. M.

Fernando de Szyszlo. *Huanacauri II*. 1964.

Fernando de Szyszlo. *Uku Pacha III – The World Beneath.* 1964.

Lima
April 20, 1965

Dear Tom Messer:

Following a common practice, you have made a kind of survey of contemporary Peruvian painting. I am not sure that this method really shows anything, though like any statistics it produces an undeniable impact.

I think that before the Peruvian situation can be fully understood, an exploration in depth is needed. My country has begun the process of winning back its true personality. The task is extremely hard, but I agree with Rilke that the artist should love difficulty. It is the price one pays for quality. Some artists – I return to the case of Szyszlo – have demonstrated remarkable insight into the essential values of Peru. Their insight has stimulated our painters to follow suit, to search out and decipher the true nature of our country.

The best of Peruvian painters are probing the soul of Peru. Adhering to an international standard, therefore, is not their true goal. I am sure that this adherence will develop in some instances, but only incidentally, when the essence of the Peruvian soul has become part of the artists' work.

I agree with you that the work of Szyszlo is of a very high order. In my judgment, he is the most important of today's Peruvian painters. When he first appeared, around 1945, the panorama of Peruvian painting was rather amorphous. The 'indigenous' school had lost its dominance, and the eyes of the young painters were turned toward the 'isms' of the Paris School. Owing to the time lag in Peru, however, these artists ended up importing concepts that were already discarded in Europe.

When Szyszlo returned from his first stay in France, he brought with him the language of nonfigurativism, his initial contribution to the liberation of Peruvian painting. His second contribution came in 1963, after he had been living a long time in contact with his native land. A show of his paintings in Lima in December of that year signaled the emergence of Peru as the central theme of his painting. Through affinity with his country, Szyszlo has refined his technique, turning it into an unobtrusive instrument of his own spiritual richness, full of the memories, landscapes, themes, and colors of Peru.

The dramatic and sumptuous qualities that are the hallmark of Szyszlo's painting belong to his own personality. It is interesting to note that as the presence of Peru has become increasingly more visible in his work, there has been less and less evidence of the dull tension which darkened his canvases, of the neurotic way he had of composing his elements. What emerges is a composition no less intense but clearer and more luminous, no less fraught with suffering but more forceful.

Sincerely,
Carlos Rodríguez Saavedra

FERNANDO DE SZYSZLO

Born in Lima, 1925, son of a Polish geographer and a Peruvian mother of Spanish-Indian descent.

A lithe, muscular man with a distinctive face and nose, gay and moody, a *bon vivant* who loves to drive his white sports car and who is much concerned with the destinies of his two sons, Vicente and Lorenzo, named after Szyszlo's first and constant idols – Vincent Van Gogh and D. H. Lawrence.

Szyszlo belonged to that small group of artists who first did abstract art on the South American continent after World War II, and he was the first abstract painter in Peru at a time when abstract painting was not well regarded on his side of the world.

'Very often we were attacked in the newspapers and magazines,' he said, 'not only by the art critics but more often by other painters – who, by the way, became "abstracts" a few years later when it was not as risky. The more common adjectives applied to my work then were "decadent", "un-Peruvian", "immoral", and the like.'

Szyszlo feels that Peru, with its incredible mountains, deserts, and colors and its fabulously rich cultural heritage, has been a basic stimulus to his painting.

'To think that we were here trying to do abstract art with the help of the discoveries of the European artists, when some centuries ago Peruvian artists were producing a highly developed, obviously autonomous, powerful art – that thought was a very explosive one. So I became involved, first spiritually, with pre-Columbian art; afterward I started to study it.

'I have never thought of taking anything directly out of that art. To be in contact with it is an important artistic experience, but you need to forget it and let it become a part of your blood.'

In his absorption with the pre-Columbian, he sometimes takes his boys to the reconstructed Inca palace, Puruchuco, near Lima. 'The thing I love most there', he says, 'is the solid, perennial, earthy quality it has. The adobe has this strange quality. It seems that people, our people, are made of it. It is tender, fragile, and yet time- and death-defeating.

'Or Machu Picchu,' he recalls. 'I've been there twice, first in 1953; then in 1964 I spent a week there. Neruda's poem describes my reactions very well. It is really a work of art: the visible meeting point of the sacred with physical matter.'

Szyszlo's small, secret studio faces the sky and the sea. He paints undisturbed, to the music of Bach and Vivaldi and of moderns like Mahler, Schoenberg, and Berg. It takes him three weeks or more to complete a painting because he is working with transparent colors over opaque ones and must wait for the latter to dry. He works on several canvases at the same time.

Life for Szyszlo in Lima is varied and pleasant. The beach is only minutes away from his studio. He and his beautiful poetess-wife, Blanca, spend much time with their boys and meet with their friends, who include architects, writers, and politicians but no painters. He also teaches art at the Catholic University in Lima.

'Mostly Peruvians buy my paintings,' he says, 'but I would guess that a third of them are bought by Latin American collectors. To my way of thinking, this is very important, since I feel that to be able to live here, I must be able to sell my paintings here.

'I don't feel isolated,' he adds, 'though I am not unaware that living in these countries we lack the stimulation that can be provided by new shows, new trends, good museums, and so forth. But by living here, I feel that I am fighting in a total way, not only artistically but politically, in every concern, to fulfill the destiny of a group. I think that we artists are needed to provide the myths for these new societies. It is a very challenging situation, because at the bottom it is a fight to find an identity that, when found, will be individual but at the same time collective.'

Fernando de Szyszlo. *Apu Kon Ticci Viracocha*. 1964.

COLOMBIA

Lima
December 23, 1964

Mrs Marta Traba
Bogotá, Colombia

Dear Marta Traba:

Despite the relative isolation of Bogotá, there is, it seems to me, considerable activity among your younger painters – activity apparently stimulated by some private and official interests. That there is an institute dedicated solely to the presentation of contemporary Latin American art and that there are occasional purchases in this same category are facts of consequence. Significant, too, is the attitude of some banks, libraries, and cultural centers, whose trustees are evidently making it a practice to place large commissions with gifted Colombian artists. Your brisk building plan, the emergence of modest collections, and what appeared to me to be a climate of fellowship in an embryonic cultural community are also welcome signs.

The attainments in contemporary Colombian painting, although not negligible, should not be confused with the lively cultural scene itself. To my mind, there are only a few among your young painters who very clearly show talent, and they therefore may appear more advanced than they are. Like their counterparts in the United States, they are typically younger artists who know what is going on in the world and who are striving to make intelligent use of their legacy.

I tend to stress the currency of their work because at one time I used to think that, given stylistic dependence, the particular model was unimportant, and that executing a work in the language of impressionism was in principle equivalent to emulating the example of Pop Art. Obviously this is not so, for the choice of a *current* form language must be judged as more honest an act than the donning of a historic garb. It would appear then that most of your younger artists are intelligently copying formal ideas and techniques that seep down from loftier heights. This is as it should be, especially if such adaptations reflect concern with current issues rather than with historic remnants.

Of those living in Colombia, Alejandro Obregón is clearly a leader. In his present stage of development, he need not borrow devices for his art. Having freed himself from the direct tutelage of others almost a decade ago and possessing a sure hand that is capable of enacting what his painter's eye perceives, he can set about the difficult task of being himself. Like Szyszlo in Peru, or Yrarrázaval in Chile, Obregón has reached a very creditable level of authenticity. His condors and his semi-abstract seascapes, his coloristic analogues of the opulent Caribbean flora, are, to be sure, extracted from the world of observed experience. But it is his apprehension of the form language of his generation – a private version of abstract expressionism – that renders his shapes and images alive and meaningful.

In closing, I should not fail to register my admiration for the art of Botero, a painter who stands at the opposite pole from Obregón. Since, however, he has lived and worked in New York for several years and since I want merely to record my impressions of my visit to Colombia, I shall make no further comment about him.

Yours sincerely,
T. M. M.

Alejandro Obregón. *The Baroque Garden*. 1965.

ALEJANDRO OBREGÓN

One of Obregón's relations was Alvaro ('El Manco') Obregón, a legendary one-armed Basque who became President of Mexico. ('Half bandit and half general,' says Alejandro.) This Obregón is a worthy descendant; in him is also visible the influence of a strong father, a wise mother, the Mediterranean Sea, an education by Scottish Jesuits, gay years in France full of love, poverty, and adventure, and the lazy but surging, the beautiful but decaying surroundings of his chosen Barranquilla.

He spoke to me in a careful and precise English, choosing his words not for effect but as if he were searching the stream of his consciousness for the most meaningful things. Sometimes it came clear, sometimes obscure, half-perceived.

'Painting is a tremendous responsibility; when I squeeze the paint out I am afraid, literally afraid.... Too much light kills color.... In violence – a chance to see and feel extreme tenderness or extreme fury. In love – the obsession for a solution of that which one can never solve.... Sun is the lightest thing in the world... always with the moon... the eclipse....'

Obregón is the male force that mesmerizes and commands love, that can never cease... can only change to hate. Three wives, four children, to all of whom he remains the life force, however distant and elusive.

His loves are all beautiful women. Now in Barranquilla his wife is Freda, a haunting Cockney beauty transplanted, a painter of great talent, according to Obregón, who stopped painting shortly after she married him. Freda is the gentle, soft-spoken mother of Mateo, a pixy boy of five, the perfect product of this union of violent contrast.

Obregón consumes life, love, and liquor in generous quantities. They burn in him with scorching flames, searing all who are near him. But out of this fire also come his paintings.

The condor, the bird of the Andes, is the central figure in over sixty murals and paintings by Obregón. He is a huge bird, brave, solitary, soaring high above the others. He is also gullible, easily trapped, and on his way to extinction.

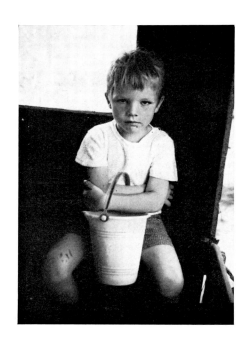

Alejandro Obregón. *The Last Condor*. 1965.

Dear Thomas Messer:

The last five years of Colombia's artistic life have been marked by startling surprises, open breaks with the strongest of traditions, rebellion of the young artists, new proposals. A culmination of the upheaval was the Primer Salón Intercol de Artistas Jóvenes, conceived and organized by the Bogotá Museum of Modern Art in 1964. In the public debate that followed, national art was rudely dissected and analyzed; there was a good deal of talk about broadening and amplifying a tradition that seemed to have been paralyzed by the veneration accorded to the Obregonian generation.

The history of Colombian art, like that of almost all other Latin American countries, has an almost linear simplicity to it. It can be fitted neatly into a general pattern that holds true for the entire continent. At the beginning of the century, painting was ruled by two equally mummifying influences: realism, as practiced by the San Fernando Academy in Madrid; and a derivative of impressionism that considered it a bold departure to work with visible brush strokes and bright or vivid colors. Next, the development of pictorial nationalism in the twenties stimulated by Mexican art, servant of the agrarian revolution. This was chronic artistic nationalism, identified with a literal interpretation of reality... and a paralysis of the search for aesthetic values, oriented toward what was provincial and transitory instead of what was central and permanent.

From 1920 to 1940, Colombia was in the grip of this restrictive nationalism. In 1940, the man who was to become our greatest national painter began to work: Alejandro Obregón. Over a period of fifteen years, Obregón perfected his style, passing through several stages of development. Underlying his style, his romantic and baroque traits – his delight in surprising and dazzling, his deep and passionate sense of painting, his conviction that a work of art must become flesh and bone – combined to strengthen his formal arguments and to define them with increasing precision. Space, color, and the building-up of forms in specified areas became the tripod, the structure on which to display proudly these underlying principles.

This powerful personality demonstrated through his work that it was possible to refer to Colombia without descending to the cheap and the commonplace. He proved that only a painting created with firm aesthetic purpose could survive in the great creative current of the century. His lesson was learned all too well. With the establishment of Obregón's prestige came the imitators – covert and overt. National art now suffers from an epidemic of romanticism. Forms become evasive; colors fade away; tiny metaphysical spaces are dropped in here and there; painted surfaces are marred by meaningless yellow drawings. When Colombian artists do things this way (in a sense, they *must* do things this way), the critics refer to the result as 'romantic expressionism'. While Obregón involuntarily has generated this pressure to conform, other artists with solid but less seductive talents – artists like Guillermo Wiedemann, Juan Antonio Roda, Eduardo Ramírez Villamizar – have carried on their work without exerting much visible influence on the new generations.

Fernando Botero, on the other hand, began to offset some of Obregón's radiance. His painting was too personal to be transformed into a 'general aesthetic' in the Obregón

Fernando Botero. *Rubens's Woman* (*La mujer de Rubens*). 1963.

fashion. But his independent stance in respect to Obregón, and to the national tendency to 'liquify' painting into a romantic-abstract disorder, marked a formidable point of divergence. Botero returned to forms their full power of expression; unlike Obregón, he gave them power and weight. He denied the transcendent notion of space and made his forms fill his canvases. By returning thus to the physical, strengthening his approach with a gigantism that poked fun at itself in an almost bloodthirsty manner, Botero dealt a severe blow to romanticism. Neither philosophy nor transcendency, nor escape, nor passion. For Botero, painting was simply a form, enormous and grotesque. Space, color, design existed as a function of form. The exaggeration of the concept of form implied a true creation, belligerent and daring. Botero was the first seriously to breach Obregón's magic universe.

The Primer Salón Intercol demonstrated the persistence of the Obregonian tradition. Even Botero's prize-winning work was a still life with fruits whose extraordinary tonal delicacy neutralized the aggressive sizes and proportions. The second prize was awarded to Nirma Zarate, an excellent young painter who has perfected the 'romantic expressionist' style. Purism and Pop Art had few followers, but there were two artists who came close to the Pop idiom: Carlos Rojas, who showed some works made with corsets and other undergarments glued on, painted white and juxtaposed against areas of solid color; and Gastón Betelli, an unknown whose huge compositions of black wood brought him a good deal of attention.

The discussion following the show made it plain that the young Colombian painters were fed up with romanticism and formal elegance and that they were eager to move in the opposite direction. They wanted to shake themselves free, to point out in some way the extent of the national crisis in which we live. They wanted to turn violent, scatological. They wanted to attack, denounce, wallow in sexuality, escape from the great national names, experiment with Pop Art, neo-figuration, the 'other' art.

Gauging the depth of this feeling, the Bogotá Museum of Modern Art decided to design its 1965 program so as to accept the challenge of the dissidents, at the same time forcing them, by showing their works, to accept full responsibility for their gestures and protests. The results have been positive beyond question. The focal field of painting has expanded. New currents are flowing, and the names one hears are no longer just Obregón and Botero but Millares, Kemeny, Dubuffet, Bacon, Karel Appel, and Rauschenberg.

The worst danger that could threaten our artistic expression is that we may convince ourselves that we have arrived at a national style, when we have only just begun to investigate the simplest happenings of national politics, economics, or local thought. The magnetism of Obregón made one think for a moment that Colombian painting *was* Obregón. The creativity of one man thus became an aesthetic postulate fitting anyone who wanted to make use of it. Today, it would appear that we have gone backward in the search for our own personality; painting has lost the apparent unity given it by Obregón, and it now seems to be torn apart by all sorts of dissimilar forces. Norman Mejía, Pablo Solano, Luis Caballero, Pedro Alcantára, and Miguel Angel Cárdenas can paint like Saura or Klee, or Bacon or Cuevas or Appel, without feeling the need to work together. However, this isn't backsliding. It is clearly a sign of sincerity after our pretense of having a common temperament to express. It is refreshing to rediscover in our young artists a leaning toward the baroque, a rejection of rules, a desperation, which in

Colombia has a fearful name: *violencia*. Violence, which is a fact (whereas romanticism is an escape), can be a fruitful motivation for Colombian art. But here we enter into the field of hypotheses.

The fact is that in Colombia there is painting of sufficiently high quality to be sent abroad. Yet the younger generation has no wish to emulate it. Rather they wish to set themselves against it and surpass it. All of this signifies that Colombian art is alive and that it has refused to slumber in provincial conformity.

Sincerely,
Marta Traba

Carlos Rojas. *Venus 65*. 1964.

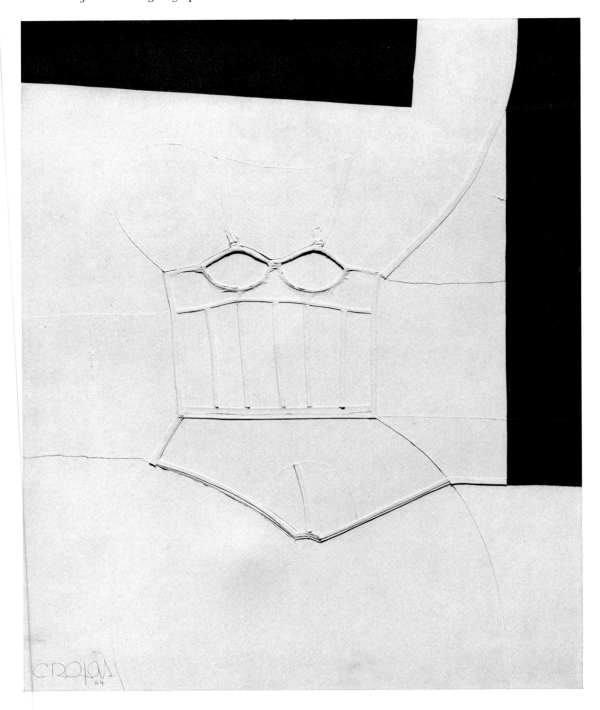

Alberto Gutiérrez. *Summa VI*. 1964.

Alberto Gutiérrez. *Summa XI*. N.D.

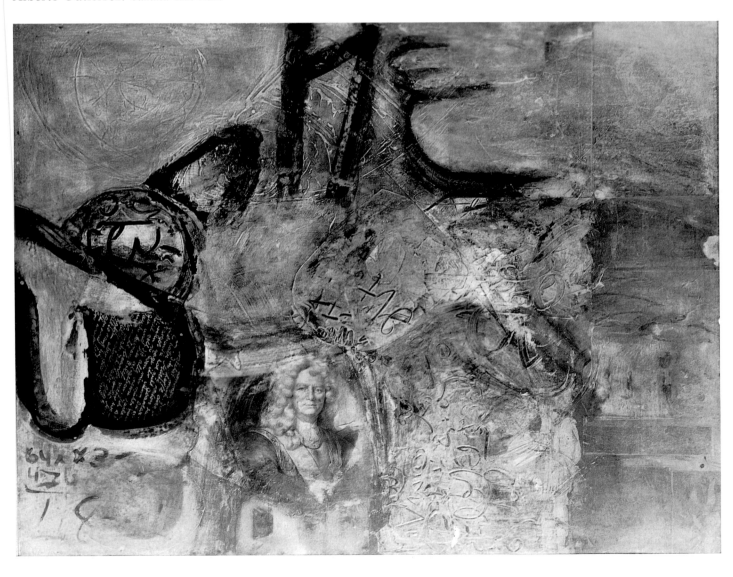

VENEZUELA

ARMANDO REVERÓN

Armando Reverón. *The Hammock (Hamaca)*. 1933.

Armando Reverón was born in Caracas on May 10, 1889, but spent his childhood in Valencia. After becoming ill with what was thought to be typhoid fever (now diagnosed as probably encephalitis), Reverón became withdrawn and aloof. From then on, eccentricity characterized his personality.

In 1904, he moved back to Caracas and entered the Academy of Fine Arts. He exhibited with Rafael Monasterios at the Music and Declamation School in Caracas in 1911. Three years later, he was granted a fellowship to travel in Europe, where he visited Barcelona, Madrid, and Paris. His work of this period shows the great influence of Spanish art.

After his return to Venezuela in 1921, Reverón moved permanently to the quiet coastal town of Macuto. His home (which he named 'the Refuge') consisted of two huts surrounded by a stone wall, and his only companion was Juanita Mota, his wife and model.

After the death of his mother in 1943, his mental condition worsened, and 1945 marked the first of his many visits to a sanitarium in Caracas. By 1952, the insanity became more pronounced and his periods of work less frequent. The following year he was admitted to a sanitarium in Caracas under the care of a psychiatrist. He stayed there until his death on September 17, 1954.

During his lifetime, Reverón had three important one-man shows. The first, held in Caracas in 1931, met with public indifference. A retrospective exhibition was held in Caracas in 1949 and a one-man show at the Centro Venezolano-Americano in Caracas. The Museum of Fine Arts, Caracas, had a memorial exhibition in 1954, and in 1956 a retrospective traveling show in the United States was organized by the Institute of Contemporary Art in Boston.

LIVING IN PAINTING: VENEZUELAN ART TODAY

Excerpts from an article by Clara Diament de Sujo

A general summing-up of conditions existing today in the contemporary arts of any one country would lack validity. Painting is not a group activity, nor the result of formal or informal associations, nor the product of specific geographic zones. It is – fortunate circumstance – the embryo of loneliness, the slow gestation of that which is unique. If at any time the best of Venezuelan art responded to a collective impulse it was during the geometric phase that won for it international prestige. But not even then did the artists yield to the impersonalization demanded by anything geometric. The paintings would isolate like axioms in the precision of angles, intersections, and sharp contours. During the process of evolution that followed, the best artists have stressed their individuality still further. Painting has thus led them, without so intending, to utterances so essentially distinct that an attempt to establish links between them would prove useless. Let us reject, therefore, the deforming vision that simply separates works of art into trends. For this may do nothing but conceal their essential values. Let us attempt instead to apprehend their uniqueness, and name that which is absolute in each artist. If we should succeed, the discerning reader will be in a better position to establish his own scale of values.

Spots of color on monochrome skies were the first stage in the work of Elsa Gramcko. Next, self-contained forms of geometric but non-Euclidian severity – monumental forms that appear to respect the flat surfaces yet throb, whirl, grow, and fold. Forms that are energy and that revel in the order of organic rhythms. An exhibition by this artist in the United States led to a series of experiences so convulsive that stroke, color, and texture burst with impulse. The forms torn from within abandon the seas of calm color, and matter henceforth knows no peace. Shaken, smashed, shattered, it resorts to incredible means in order to reveal its essence. The heightening of the process forces her to use everything within her grasp. She uses sawdust and cement, oxides and nitric acid, even the sides of an abandoned jeep found among the rocks by the sea. Amazement before the lights and colors nurtured by chemicals compels her to forget traditional paints. In the alchemy by which oxides and acids resolve their attractions and repulsions, greens, blues, reds, ochres, and grays meet in revelation. Possessed, she cannot but allow the work to come about in its irrepressible way. Until, in a work such as 'Blue Ogive', the full evolution becomes manifest. That is, the geometric thinking, the conflict with matter, the clear constructive orders, light made substance corroding and caressing, all reach a feeling of total integration; of coherence and expressiveness. For those who believe that inner affinity may be exposed, naming de Staël, Burri, Gramcko would have definite meaning.

Jesús Soto is what Merleau-Ponty calls the *phenomenal hand* which possesses, with the power of gesture alone, the law of self-realization, revealing in its passage the world of perception and motion. In the simplicity of one step alone, Soto elucidates the infinite sum of spaces and instants. It was always like this. From his very first compositions with geometric elements the forms trapped in taut shapes made light vibrate and time-spaces elapse. How is the awareness of motion born in an artist? How are impulses released into space? What determines that magic, undeviating drift of light, color, and time fleeing from the panels to the surrounding atmosphere? Not even Soto knows the answer. He once took a wire in his hands and made it into a knot, a tangle, as if wishing to impose a given course upon it. Each time the fine wire would react in a different way. The feeling of all that exists was projected with infinite momentum. Thus new works by Soto have won enthusiastic recognition in Venice, Kassel, and New York. In these *Vibrations*, spaces of time jump, cross, and turn before a lineal surface and toss themselves as lightning in one stroke that holds all strokes. It is an unbearable apprehension while the impending move is born and reborn, made and unmade in time and space, pregnant with meaning, leaving no trace bold enough to re-enact the elapsed. We may approach the intuition of worlds in the work of art but we cannot hold it. The sense of the absolute may be discerned, never expressed, and least of all nailed to a cross of words borne with other burdens.

In Alejandro Otero the motivation of his human attitude and the intelligence of what he says and writes respond to deep expressive urges. The progression that marks his work is evidence of the cohesion of this artistic thought. No one has dared to make changes more drastic than he. Figurative stages that signified experiences in depth broke into a series of white canvases scarcely illuminated with color that required a lapse of fifteen years before being shown. Also left behind was a rich perspective of color-rhythms conceived in the geometric relation of space-forms to light-spaces, as well as multiple stages in the search for new links between things. An inner elation has determined the areas of communication where the cleavage appears to be. For it is here that Otero questions the visible, demands to know its secret. It is here that he faces the decisive moment when *living as a painter* he discovers a unity without return. It is as if the expression had exposed itself to put forward the being that had to be. In no work by Otero is the spirit of classicism absent. One should speak of style to express the bond between the diverse stages which compose the work of this artist. Revealed in every one of his gestures, style is born unintended, as evident to others as it is invisible to himself. It can only be born of the deepest inner truth, for there is no formula to bring it into the world. Style will invade the gesture only of the creator who avoids it.

All truth is simple. Truth brings light to the soul and peace to the spirit. The work of Leufert has never been a dense jungle of hermetic meanings. Always luminous, woven of brilliancies and opacities, total hues and snatches of light, his wide, beautiful canvases are himself. The spontaneous activity of the imagination extricates the essence of individual being. The land of symbols does not exist for Leufert. For his nature is one of contemplation. At the present time, vibrations of color and light, rather than form, introduce a different causality. In the work born after his long sojourn in New York a decisive power has begun to tear itself away from the dense zones of color. The signs emerging from the mystic element that runs through his work refuse all symbolism, while evoking what is at one time distant and deep....

'We are the world,' says Jaimes-Sánchez in his paintings. We cannot think with the eyes, nor without them. Vision informs and provides the clues to our intuition. For many years an abstract-impressionist attitude made him paint psychological landscapes endowed with rare human quality. Everything happened in the world of perception and gesture that bred in him the wonder of creation. Those who may have followed the slow gestation of the work of this artist, witnessed his doubts, his self-questioning, will welcome his latest works. That which seemed to hinder him – his passion for life, his intuition of limiting forces, his feelings of guilt and inadequacy – now made a way for him. The conversion is completed. The artist is what he thinks and what he wants to be. Air-drawn daggers from the past, the absurd, the imaginary will bring in visions of a world that transcends its limitations. To go from life to life is to have no face of one's own. When visions such as these interweave fact and fancy, object and dream-object, experience and hope, they provide findings that enrich the culture of peoples....

New York
May 14, 1965

Mrs Clara de Sujo
Caracas, Venezuela

Dear Clara de Sujo:

I intended to write to you after my return from Venezuela in January to obtain your views on the present state of Venezuelan painting. However, your very interesting article in *Art International* made your views clear, so that it seems preferable here to relate the pertinent passages quoted to the occasion at hand.

A word about your choice of artists first: I am sure that you arrived at the selection after much thought and after exercising to the full your intimate knowledge of the Venezuelan scene. It is equally clear from your expressed attitude toward selective processes that you do not intend the choice to be exclusive and permanent but that it merely reflects one of a number of possible valid alternatives and one that is subject to re-evaluation. I have gone to some pains to make similar allowances for my exhibition choices.

As it happens, your selections and mine are not far apart. This is understandable if one considers that, though they were arrived at separately, they were made at about the same time and within the limited range of a single country. To compare notes: we have both taken a special interest in Soto, Jaimes-Sánchez, Elsa Gramcko, and Leufert. Your article also deals sympathetically with the work of Otero and others. Some of these I had considered carefully and finally eliminated with regret in order to stay within an exhibition scope that was determined, among other things, by questions of size, continental balance, and other extrinsic factors. I should like to stress that my exclusion of Otero, surely one of Venezuela's finest artists, was done only after much soul-searching and by agreement with Otero himself, who wished to withhold public showing of his most recently conceived, and still in many ways tentative, departures. This leaves Reverón, who is clearly beyond the scope of your article and whom I feature by way of introduction, and Borges, whose strong semifigurative contemporary expressionism has special meaning to me.

Jacobo Borges. *Personage of the Coronation (Personaje de la coronación)*. 1963.

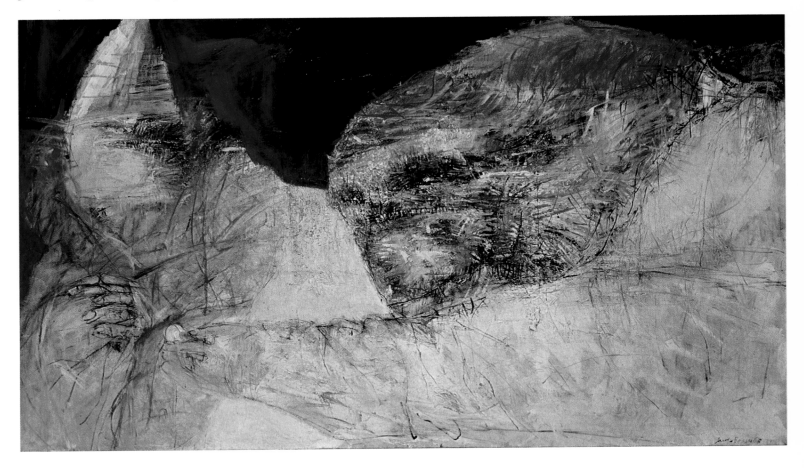

Apart from the selection, your article raises other issues which it would be rewarding to discuss at some length. For the moment, let me say that you go somewhat further than I would in rejecting art as a group activity and in endorsing its validity as the 'slow gestation of that which is unique'. The question of uniqueness that you raise would seem to need some qualification. In a sense, all art is unique. Yet at the same time an expression that has the appearance of unrelatedness to existing modes is exceedingly rare since it must be founded upon the exceptional capacity to absorb existing modes and to go beyond them. Therefore, painting today, or at any time for that matter, far from being stylistically unique, must be seen as existing within broad premises *previously* established. The question is how true, how personally valid for the artist, and, therefore, how rewarding and pertinent for the viewer. The gestation that you speak of takes place within a soil fertilized by known ingredients that the artist and, in any case, the critic, cannot afford to ignore.

In saying this I realize that our difference of emphasis is partly a semantic one. I also know your aversion to trend-thinking and to the tendency to judge styles and idioms in qualitative terms – as if any 'ism' in itself could be good or bad, artistically valid or not. In this, I am thoroughly in agreement with you.

With best regards,
T. M. M.

Humberto Jaimes-Sánchez. *After 1913 'Study'*
(*Después de 1913 'Estudio'*). 1964.

Elsa Gramcko. *The White Castle* (*El castillo blanco*). N.D.

Alejandro Otero. *In Manuscript, Brown and Silver*
(*En manuscrito, marrón y plata*). 1963.

Alejandro Otero. *In Manuscript and Silver*
(*En manuscrito y plata*). N.D.

Gerd Leufert. *Betijoque.* 1964.

Humberto Jaimes-Sánchez. *I Love your Crazy Years*
(*Amo tus años locos*). N.D.

Francisco Hung. *Rain-making Machine* (*Máquina creadora de lluvia*). 1963.

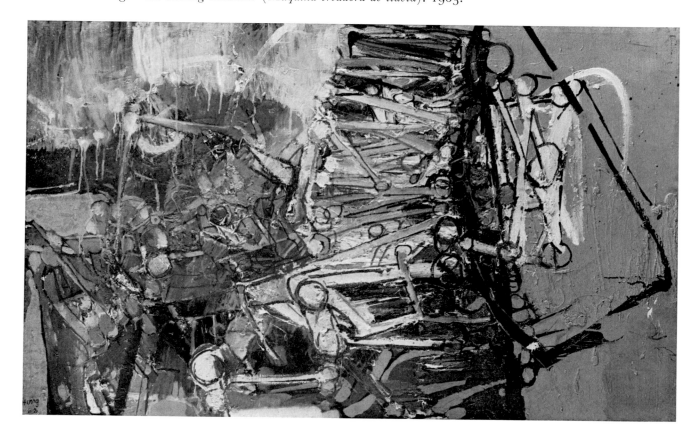

Luisa Richter. *Landscape* (*Paisaje*). 1964.

EXPATRIATES: PARIS

Judging by the number of artists who make the pilgrimage to Paris, the French capital still remains the Mecca for Latin American painters. Because of this fact, a European rather than a North American aesthetic orientation prevails in almost all the Latin American art centers. It is de Staël and Dubuffet, Tàpies and Jorn, rather than Pollock and de Kooning, Rothko and Newman, who are used most frequently as models in the art centers of Caracas, Buenos Aires, São Paulo, and Santiago.

It was within the stimulating ambience of the younger generation of the School of Paris that Venezuela's Soto developed his early awareness of a kinetic and optical potential. A significant contribution to the Nouvelle Tendance form of early Op Art came from a group of young Argentine expatriates.

The Musée d'Art Moderne de la Ville de Paris took cognizance of this influx in the summer of 1965 by arranging a large show that revealed the breadth of the current as well as its impurities.

SOTO

'Paris is delicious to a painter!'

Soto referred not only to his present life but to the early days, fifteen years before, when he arrived in Paris from his native Venezuela.

Paris was just recovering from the war, and Soto liked the Parisians immediately: 'In this city, even if you have no name but people know that you are an artist, there is warmth.... They accord you a small distinction and respect.'

He made his living playing the guitar ('the most intimate of all instruments') in Left Bank night clubs, especially in one called L'Escale, founded by some Latin American painters. Even now Soto occasionally drops in and cannot resist joining the other guitars.... 'I used to get twenty francs a night, and beer was only a franc a glass,' Soto recalls nostalgically.

His purpose, though, was serious. At twenty-seven he had already earned a reputation as an accomplished painter in Venezuela, but he had felt isolated there. He wanted a change, wanted to integrate his work, and wanted to learn about the state of painting after cubism.

'I knew that there had to be "something", but apart from the knowledge of Picasso's evolution, I did not know what it was.'

In his search, Soto became deeply absorbed in the work of Mondrian and Calder.

'I saw how Calder integrated time and movement in sculpture and I wanted to do the same thing in painting.... I tried to make Mondrian's elements move on canvas.'

Eight months after his arrival in Paris, Soto exhibited six of his works in the Salon de Réalité Nouvelle and so started a new form in the evolution of painting, the 'Optical Vibration'. These six paintings were, incidentally, the last Soto did on canvas. He moved on to 'Optical Relief', and many exhibitions followed.

Soto's life was not all painting, however. He courted and married a Parisienne, Helène, a medical researcher, and the Sotos now have four bright and loving children. They live in the historic Marais district of Paris, on the rue de Turennes. The apartment is large and airy and full of Soto's 'Vibrations' from different periods. On the fourth floor (a walk-up, of course) in the same building is Soto's tiny, well-ordered studio, which has the appearance of a carpenter shop.

'I always work regularly,' Soto said. 'At noon, my little girl comes and calls me to eat and I descend. We eat, I play the guitar a little and then return to work until the sun goes down and I feel like stopping.'

Soto's work is slow and painstaking. A large piece takes a week to do. As he leaned over, making his characteristic white lines over the black background, I was reminded of a medieval monk working on his hand-illuminated Bible, a work of deep belief and supreme patience.

Curiously enough, living in Paris brought Soto nearer to his native Venezuela. 'I have grown closer and closer to Venezuela because of the interest there in my paintings. Now I have a plan to create a museum in my home town, Ciudad Bolívar, filled with my own work and that of other *avant-garde* artists. I have exchanged, bought, and am being given work for this purpose, and with the help of many art patrons there I hope to start building a small museum – three or four rooms at first and expand later – to be ready within the next two years.'

Soto is deeply concerned with the evolution of painting and with his own role in it. 'I have great respect for Mondrian, for Kandinsky and Malewitch. They prepared us for Optical Art, eliminating visual concepts of the classical Greek and of the Renaissance. I believe that my contribution consists of having integrated movement in painting, using the vision of man as the motor.'

Paris has given Soto what he had hoped it would: a new understanding, a role in the evolution of painting.

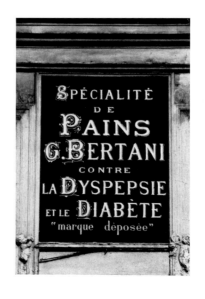

Jesús Rafael Soto. *Vibration* (*Vibración*). 1965.

MEXICO

RUFINO TAMAYO

When Olga and Rufino Tamayo celebrated their thirty-second wedding anniversary recently, they transformed the garden of their Mexico City home into a fairyland of colored lights and gave a costume ball. Tamayo wore a beautiful ceremonial samurai costume which the Japanese government had given him after his triumphant show in Japan. With 250 'intimate friends' the Tamayos sang, danced, and drank French champagne until dawn.

'Thirty-two years ago,' reminisces Olga, 'we went to New York moneyless, on the bus. The trip took seven days. When we arrived, Rufino took me right from the bus station to Fifty-seventh Street and said, 'Look, Olga, New York is the capital of the world. This is Fifty-seventh Street, which has the best galleries, the best art. Nobody knows me here, but I promise you one thing: one day all these galleries will want my work!'

Tamayo recalls, 'I wanted to be in New York, a modern city in a modern age, a modern concept. The time I struggled there was my best, when I wanted to be recognized. And when all doors opened, that was exciting too!'

The doors began to open when he took his gouaches to Julien Levy, who immediately gave him a show following one of Salvador Dali's work in the same gallery.

'I am an international painter – not nationalistic at all,' Tamayo says. 'I'm glad to have my paintings all over the world, to have them seen and understood by many. I want to have shows wherever I have not been shown – New York, Paris, Zurich – everywhere.

'I adore New York. My best friends are there, and it is the center of things. But being away from Mexico does not change my being Mexican. I have lived abroad, but my heart belongs here, and I always come home. I have very strong roots. I like Mexico City, the climate, my house. I love to touch the earth, love the smell of the garden, love the animals and the flowers. It is the ground that counts most here.'

Tamayo now spends his time at home, except when he goes to attend the openings of his exhibits. Vigorous in movement, he paints steadily in his modern, simple studio which opens onto his garden, where he plants flowers and trees, whistles with his birds, and is surrounded by stone mementoes of his Mexican-Indian heritage.

There are usually luncheon guests, but Tamayo is relatively undisturbed – Olga sees to that.

'I am a housewife, secretary, and everything else,' she says. 'I enjoy helping him with all that he hates to do, so that he can paint. My children are Tamayo's paintings.'

Tamayo on painting: 'I regard it as a trade, in which you have to exercise your technique every day. I work steadily, regularly, from 10 A.M. until it gets dark, and never with artificial light....

'Painting is an invention. A painter has to know all techniques. I am not particularly interested in mural painting, but it is part of my job. Murals are restricting. Portraits must be like their subjects. In easel painting, though, I am 100 per cent free and can experiment....

'My ideas are purely plastic. Art has to be humanistic. My theme is man – man confronted with happenings.... Somehow when a painting is finished, it is dead, like a corpse. I must start all over again.'

Tamayo works five days in Mexico City and relaxes on weekends at his home in Cuernavaca. 'I want to concentrate when I work,' he says, 'and I want to have fun after. Having fun is invigorating and I like doing what others do. I am part of the world. I am no different from other men.

'This is the time for the arts. In the olden times you had to die in order to be recognized. Look around here – I live well, and my best painting is the one I will do next. I am renewing myself each time.'

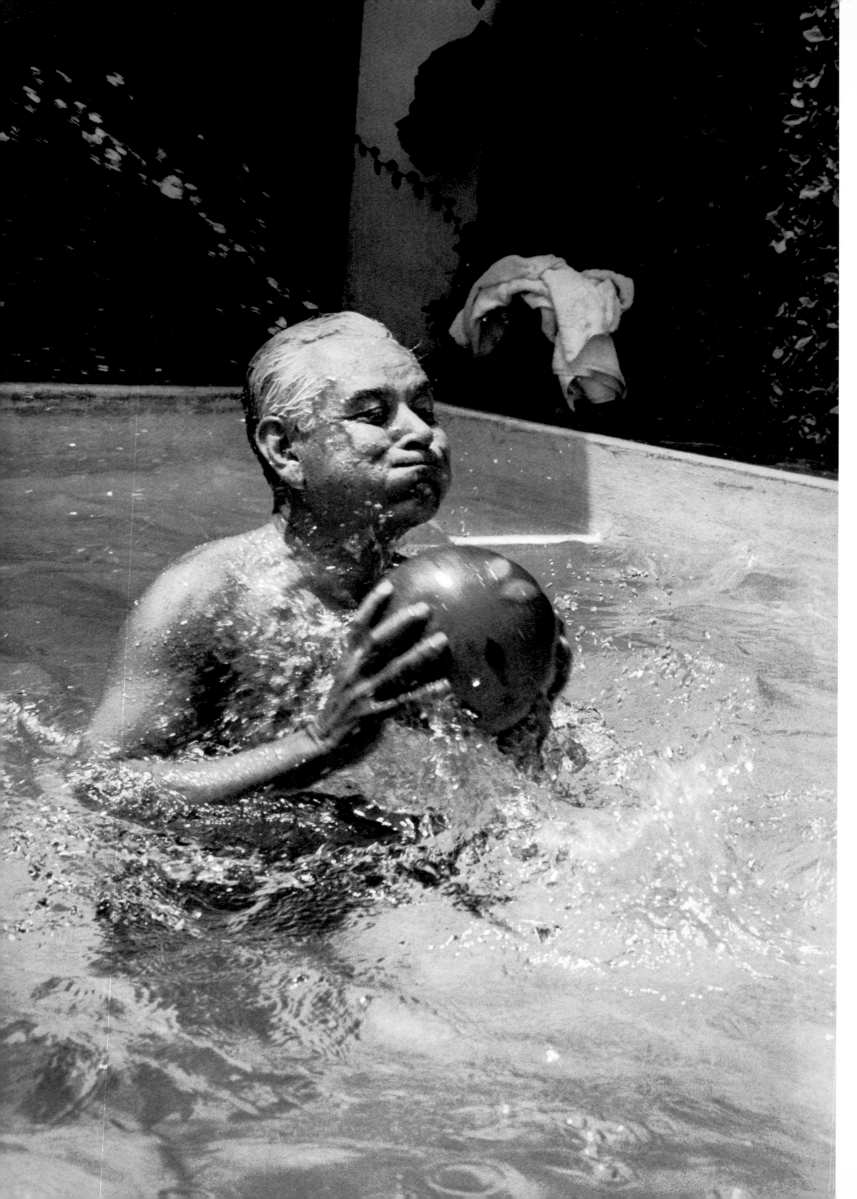

Rufino Tamayo. *Portrait of his Wife*. 1964.

Bogotá
December 5, 1964

Mr Mathias Goeritz
Mexico City, Mexico

Dear Mathias:

To a lesser extent than in Argentina, but more than anywhere else in Latin America, I found in Mexico a climate in which the contemporary artist can live and work. The arts, of course, are an old story with you in Mexico, but the case of Peru shows that it does not follow that they need be a new story as well. Perhaps the existence of an intermediate phase (that of your Mexican school), for which there is no Peruvian counterpart, accounts for the difference. Probably owing to these earlier exertions, art (and painting in particular) is more official and more readily accepted than elsewhere in Latin America. The blessing, however, it seems to me, is mixed, partly because your great triad – Orozco, Rivera, and Siqueiros – now seems so uneven. Powerful and clearly inspirational at their best, they seem unbelievably poor and deficient at their worst. Notwithstanding their revolutionary zeal and their courage that led them to translate a dated iconography into pertinent and, in their day, contemporary images, their claim to formal innovation is dubious. For it is clear that the best of Dr Atl's landscapes have their stylistic roots in European Art Nouveau (those Hodler mountains and those remarkably Klimtian portraits), while Orozco adopted for himself (with intelligence and understanding) the form language of German expressionism. As for Rivera and Siqueiros, again without wishing to deny their mural attainments, one cannot miss their eclectic – I would almost say, opportunist – evolution or lose sight of the fact that some of the worst canvases bear their signature. It is open to argument, therefore, how much your grand old men contributed in artistic substance and qualitative example, although the victorious battle they waged for art, in general, has certainly helped to create the favorable environment that I mention at the outset of this letter.

Two artists of two subsequent generations, however, seem to me to have great merit. Both exert considerable influence in your country and beyond the geographic limits of Mexico. I am referring to Tamayo among the old and to Cuevas among the young artists.

Tamayo's one-man show was installed at your newly inaugurated Museo Nacional de Arte Moderno and gave me a very welcome insight into the art of your leading modern painter. I thought remarkable the degree to which he had overcome the originally impeding heritage of cubism (that great albatross around the neck of Latin American painters) and the way his most subtle color combines with increasingly expressive forms to create some memorable works. Moreover, in Latin America, Tamayo is the leading exponent among those who attain an indigenous expression from within, i.e. through the formal substances of his work, rather than from without, through the ineffective and unconvincing approach via programmatic subject-matter. In Mexico, no one before Tamayo, nor anyone after him to the same degree, has been capable of achieving such native strength through (paradoxically) such highly sophisticated means. No wonder therefore that Tamayo's forms evoke strong echoes inside and outside of Mexico and that contemporary painting abounds with inane imitations as well as with reasoned and valid deductions.

Cuevas, totally different from Tamayo and much younger, has a potential that seems quite exceptional by any standard. His work speaks to me with the utmost clarity, integrity, and conviction. Although Cuevas may inherit Tamayo's mantle, he will do so by having planted the Judas kiss of total rejection upon the older artist's cheek. For not only does he avoid Tamayo's reliance upon color by staying within an essentially graphic framework but he also rejects cubism as a point of departure by establishing a direct line with a pre-modern idiom. Cuevas is young enough to bypass Picasso in order to draw nourishment from the rich soil of Goya's graphic work. As with Tamayo, following this path also leads to an authentic national expression, though, in keeping with his specific artistic organism, it uncovers and illuminates entirely different facets of a complex national physiognomy.

Evaluation becomes more difficult as we pass to the area of emerging talent. Pedro Coronel, an artist of solid attainment, seems on the verge of flight. For the moment his wings are still confined by regional fetters. Rafael, his younger brother, is more imaginative but less developed. His forms are thin and his Mexican expressionism lacks weight. Corvas, Gironella, Toledo, and a number of others bear watching, but I have seen too little of their work – and that of Belkin and Icaza – to form a clear opinion of it.

In general, the contemporary Mexican scene seems in flux. The immensely gifted Cuevas has created images that are convincing in his own work but that become easily subject to mere pictorialization in the hands of others endeavoring to use them. The mine that Cuevas struck, however, is a rich one and no one can foretell what further strata lie below those already uncovered. For the time being, then, youthful efforts in Mexico are groping, and no clear direction has emerged from an evidently intensive search and from a promising variety of experimental departures. Or at least my brief confrontation with Mexican painting failed to reveal one. Perhaps you think differently about these issues.

Sincerely,
T. M. M.

José Luis Cuevas. *Page with Ancestors*. N.D.

José Luis Cuevas. *The Printmaker Désandré Working on a Self-portrait.* 1965.

José Luis Cuevas. *Joan of Arc with Two Fat Personages*. 1963.

José Luis Cuevas. *The Idiot and his Sisters*. 1963.

Paris
April 27, 1965

Dear Tom Messer:

From the general point of view of an art critic, one has to agree with what you say about the 'Mexican School' painters. But should we judge these artists by aesthetic standards when their aim has been in a different direction?

For most people, of course, art and aesthetics are the same. Because they are, all kinds of works end up in museums or other institutions, where they are classified as good, middling, or bad art. But being a sculptor and painter myself, I find that I revolt against the conversion of the Mexican social or political message into 'gallery' art, much as I revolt against the hanging of Dada manifestations in a museum. The Mexican Mural Movement was somehow like Dada – an attempt to put an end to the useless creed of *l'art pour l'art*. It was doomed to failure because of its spiritual limitations. But still one cannot deny that these revolutionary painters were searching for a function in art, an approach that makes the whole movement unusually interesting.

One might say that in a way these men, especially Rivera and Alfaro Siqueiros, were the forerunners of modern Pop Art in the United States. I do not think that the works of Lichtenstein, Segal, or Warhol appeal because of their aesthetic values.

Now that the old revolutionary spirit has gone, some critics have unearthed new and specious arguments to defend their heroes. It has become fashionable to attack Rivera and Siqueiros and to defend José Clemente Orozco as a 'better' painter than his colleagues. Some people have taken to praising Rivera's cubist period. (I personally have the impression that Rivera did not entirely understand why he was painting in that manner.)

Of course, with Tamayo the whole situation changed. Tamayo is an excellent painter. His painting is a completely different affair, and I agree with what you say about him. The few paintings of earlier years, when he tried to go along with the revolutionary tradition, are not very convincing. Certainly, for Mexico, Tamayo is of great importance. His work means a liberation from all kinds of complexes. (To me personally, his work is – like most 'good modern painting' – rather boring; I prefer the ugliness of our 'pre-Pop' artists.)

You are right to complain about the confusion in the Mexican art world of today. The facts are that the revolution is over and that we live in a kind of socialized democracy. The Mexican artists nowadays are divided, working in many directions – just as is true elsewhere. The only difference is that in your country, when the museums become interested in a new development, it automatically becomes fashionable. Mexico City does not have the powerful, privately owned, *avant-garde* taste-makers that you have in New York. Our modern art museum has been open for about a year, but it is run by the good old National Fine Arts Institute. The Institute is becoming rather abstract-minded (of course, it is at least ten years behind the times). But in spite of all kinds of public protests by some artists, everyone seems more or less happy with the situation. The once quasi-official Revolutionary School is still selling its murals, though mostly in the provinces, I believe. In Mexico City, Tamayo has become the high priest, and the big prizes now – for a change – are going into the pockets of 'abstract' painters, though it is true that only a very limited number of intellectuals like this kind of art.

In sum, our arts reflect our heterogeneous society. Isn't this true all over the world?

Actually, I think we have quite a few talented artists. Siqueiros and Tamayo are still around. There is an 'in-between' generation, an interesting and unstudied chapter in Mexican art, with artists like Ricardo Martínez and Juan Soriano. There is Cuevas, a young genius whose work I admire as much as you and perhaps more. There are the so-called 'insiders' who try to follow Cuevas's tendencies. More recently some late-blooming 'abstract expressionists' and neo-surrealist-assemblage artists have turned up.

Carlos Mérida and Gunther Gerzo are our most outstanding painters of hard-edge abstracts. We have an extremely gifted outsider who moves between a kind of architectural surrealism, Pop, and Op: Pedro Friedeberg. There are, in the crafts, some international talents like the weaver Sheila Hicks and the ceramist Jorge Wilmont. We even have 'los hartos' – those who are fed up with all this 'art' nonsense. I belong to that group.

Finally, one should not forget that in the relationship of the arts to architecture, Mexico is still more active than many other countries, thanks to the astonishing number of architects interested in this question: Luis Barragán, Félix Candela, Ricardo Legorreta, Mario Pani, Ricardo de Robina, and others.

As I look back over the list, things don't seem so bad to me, though I guess you would expect still more.

Sincerely,
Mathias Goeritz

Rafael Coronel. *Head (Cabeza)*. 1964.

160

Ricardo Martínez. *Reclining Figure* (*Figura yacente*). 1963.

Ricardo Martínez. *Seated Man* (*Hombre sentado*). 1964.

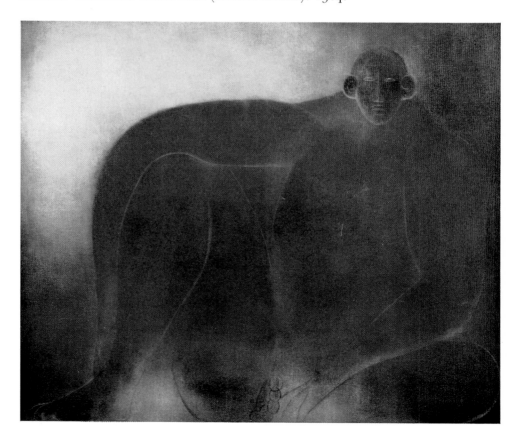

Alberto Gironella. *Obrados.* 1964.

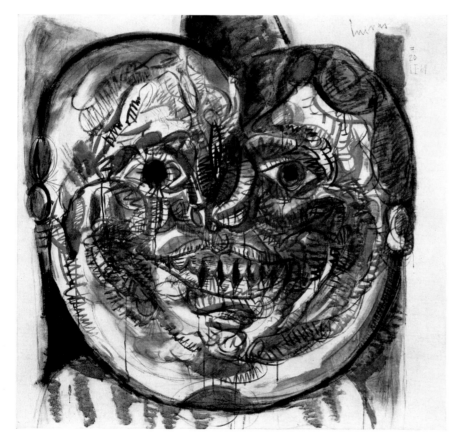

José Luis Cuevas. *The Marquis de Sade as a Boy*
(*Marquís de Sade niño*). N.D.

Pedro Coronel. *Man of Broken Dreams*
(*El hombre de los sueños rotos*). 1964.

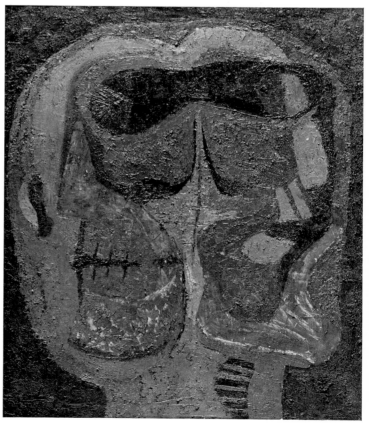

Pedro Coronel. *Opaque Pain* (*Dolor opaco*). 1964.

POSTSCRIPT

The eighth Bienal at São Paulo with its heavy representation of Latin American painting affords a favorable opportunity to make some revisions of judgment and to qualify some earlier statements. Qualification seems all the more desirable since a year has passed between the time of the selection and the exhibition's first presentation and since more time will elapse before the show completes its scheduled itinerary.

In general, visits to the national sections representing the Latin American republics lead to confirmation of previous impressions. Argentina remains by far the most accomplished among Latin American countries. Her painters have given further impressive evidence of ability. Venezuela, whose vitality as an arts center has been previously noted, has also moved forward, if we may judge from an extremely successful showing of three young Venezuelan painters, each of whom is excellent within the range of his work. The showing of Brazilian and Mexican painters at the Bienal confirms an impression of active involvement and uneven accomplishment. Among nations formerly depending upon the excellence of a single artist, Peru shows the clearest advance at the Bienal.

In the assessment of individual contributions, a few corrections are necessary. The huge Brazilian section has confirmed Marc Berkowitz's remark to me that 'there are, of course, a great many artists whose work you have apparently not seen.... I think that they are at least as important as some of the artists you mentioned.' I also must note the relatively weak showing of Serpa and the impressive group of recent paintings by Manabu Mabe, who, despite his failings, remains an authoritative painter when attentive to his work. One should also mention the one-man show dedicated to Yolanda Mohalyi, who, in her most recent paintings, clearly transcends the limitations pointed out in the earlier correspondence. Finally, the two artists who at the Bienal more than justified previous favorable assessments are Polesello of Argentina and Borges of Venezuela.

SELECTED BIOGRAPHIES

A limited and, to a degree, arbitrary choice has determined entries in the following biographical presentation. In general, older artists of established reputation have been given priority.

ARGENTINA

José Antonio Fernández-Muro
Born 1920, Madrid. Moved to Argentina, 1938. First one-man show, Galería Witcomb, Buenos Aires, 1944. UNESCO fellowship to study museology in Europe and United States, 1957–1958. Resident New York since 1962.

Sarah Grilo
Born 1920, Buenos Aires. Lived in Madrid and Paris, 1948–1950. First one-man show, Galería Palma, Madrid, 1949. Traveled in Europe and United States, 1957–1958. Fellowship, John Simon Guggenheim Memorial Foundation, 1962. Resident New York since 1962.

Kazuya Sakai
Born 1921, Buenos Aires. Studied in Japan, 1934–1951. Professor of Oriental Philosophy, Universidad Nacional de Tucumán, Argentina. Member, Orient-Occident Committee, UNESCO, Argentina. First one-man show, Galería Bonino, Buenos Aires, 1952. Gold Medal Award, Brussels World's Fair, 1958. Resident New York since 1963.

Miguel Ocampo
Born 1922, Buenos Aires. Studied architecture; began painting in 1944. Resident Paris, 1949–1950. First one-man show, Galerie Ariel, Paris, 1950. Cultural Attaché, Argentine Embassy, Paris, 1956–1959. Resident Paris as Cultural Attaché, Argentine Embassy.

Clorindo Testa
Born 1923, Naples. Family moved to Argentina, 1924. Studied architecture, Universidad de Buenos Aires. Traveled in Spain and Italy, 1949–1951. First one-man show, Galería Van Riel, Buenos Aires, 1952. First Prize, Instituto Torcuato Di Tella, Buenos Aires, 1961. Resident Buenos Aires.

Ernesto Deira
Born 1928, Buenos Aires. Graduate, law degree, Universidad de Buenos Aires, 1950. Studied in Europe, 1953, 1962. First one-man show, Galería Witcomb, Buenos Aires, 1960. Resident Buenos Aires.

Jorge de la Vega
Born 1930, Buenos Aires. Studied architecture for six years, Universidad de Buenos Aires. First one-man show, Banco Municipal de Buenos Aires, 1951. Studied in Europe, 1962. Teaches visual appreciation at Universidad de Buenos Aires. Resident Buenos Aires.

Martha Peluffo
Born 1931, Buenos Aires. First one-man show, Galería Antú, Buenos Aires, 1952. Purchase Prize at the VII° Bienal de São Paulo, 1963. Resident Buenos Aires.

Rómulo Macció
Born 1931, Buenos Aires. Graphic artist who has worked in advertising agencies since 1945. First one-man show, Galería Galatea, Buenos Aires, 1956. Studied in Europe, 1961, 1963, on fellowship from Instituto Torcuato Di Tella, Buenos Aires. Resident Paris since 1963.

Luis Felipe Noé
Born 1933, Buenos Aires. Studied with Horatio Butler, 1952. First one-man show, Galería Witcomb, Buenos Aires, 1959. Studied in Paris, 1961, on French Government fellowship; in United States, 1964, on fellowship from Instituto Torcuato Di Tella. Resident Buenos Aires.

Rogelio Polesello
Born 1939, Buenos Aires. Graduate of Escuela Nacional de Bellas Artes, Buenos Aires, 1958. First one-man show, Galería Peuser, Buenos Aires, 1959. Resident Buenos Aires.

BRAZIL

Flávio de Rezende Carvalho
Born 1899, Rio de Janeiro. Studied at Lycée Janson de Sailly, Paris. Studied in England at Stonyhurst College, University of Durham, Clapham College, King Edward the Seventh School of Fine Arts. First one-man show, São Paulo, 1932. Author of many books and articles. Resident São Paulo.

Sergio Iberê Camargo
Born 1914, Restinga Sêca, Rio Grande do Sul. Studied at Escola de Belas Artes, Rio de Janeiro. Studied in Europe, 1947. Studied painting with di Chirico and Lhote. First one-man show, Ministry of Education, Rio de Janeiro, 1946. Resident Rio de Janeiro.

Iván Serpa
Born 1923, Rio de Janeiro. Studied in Brazil with Leskochek. Studied in Europe, 1958. First one-man show, Instituto Brasil – Estados Unidos, Rio de Janeiro, 1951. Named best young Brazilian painter at the I° Bienal de São Paulo, 1951. Teaches drawing and painting, Museu de Arte Moderna, Rio de Janeiro. Resident Rio de Janeiro.

Raimundo de Oliveira
Born 1930, Feira de Santana, Bahia, Brazil. First one-man show, Feira de Santana, 1951–1953. Died January 1966 in Bahia.

Tomoshige Kusuno
Born 1935, city of Yubari, state of Hokkaido, Japan. First one-man exhibition, Sanshodo Gallery, Tokyo, 1955. Emigrated to Brazil, 1960. Esso Salon, and VIII° Bienal de São Paulo, 1965. Resident São Paulo.

CHILE

Matta (Roberto Sebastián Antonio Matta Echaurren)
Born 1912, Santiago. Graduate, School of Architecture, Santiago, 1933. Studied with Le Corbusier, Paris, 1934–1937. Began painting in surrealist style, 1937. Moved to New York, 1939. First one-man show, Julien Levy Gallery, New York, 1940. Resident Paris.

Ricardo Yrarrázaval
Born 1931, Santiago. Studied in Rome, 1952. Académie Julian, Paris, 1953. First one-man show, Santiago, 1954. Resident Santiago.

Enrique Castrocid
Born 1937, Santiago. Studied at School of Fine Arts, Santiago, 1957–1959. First one-man show, Santiago, 1960. Recipient of O.A.S. Fellowship to study in New York, 1962. Recipient of John Simon Guggenheim Memorial Foundation Fellowship, 1964. Resident New York.

COLOMBIA

Alejandro Obregón
Born 1920, Barcelona. Moved to Barranquilla, Colombia. Attended Boston School of Fine Arts, 1937–1941. First one-man show, El Caballito, Bogotá, 1947. Director, Escuela de Bellas Artes, Bogotá, 1948–1949 and 1959–1960. Went to France in 1949. Resident Barranquilla.

Fernando Botero
Born 1932, Medellín, Colombia. Studied painting in Madrid, 1952; in Paris, 1953; Accademia San Marco, Florence, 1954. First one-man show, Bogotá, 1951. First-prize winner, Bienal de Barcelona, 1955. Guggenheim National Prize of Colombia, 1960. Resident New York.

MEXICO

Rufino Tamayo
Born 1899, Oaxaca, Mexico. Attended Academía de San Carlos, Mexico City, 1917. First one-man show, Weyhe Gallery, New York, 1926. Professor of Painting, Instituto Nacional de Bellas Artes, Mexico City. Moved to New York City, 1938. Painted murals for Smith College Library, Northampton, Massachusetts, 1943; National Palace of Fine Arts, Mexico City, 1952. Traveled extensively in United States and Europe. Resident Mexico City.

Ricardo Martínez
Born 1918, Mexico City. Graduate of the University of Mexico. First one-man show, Galería de Arte Mexicano, Mexico City, 1944. Only artist chosen to represent Mexico at VIIº Bienal de São Paulo, 1963. Resident Mexico City.

Pedro Coronel
Born 1922, Zacatecas, Mexico. Studied at La Esmeralda School of Painting and Sculpture, Mexico City, 1940. Studied in Europe with Brauner and Brancusi. Winner of Orozco Prize, Segunda Bienal, Mexico, 1960.

José Luis Cuevas
Born 1933, Mexico City. First one-man show, Donceles Street, Mexico City, 1947. Visiting Professor, School of Art of the Museum of Philadelphia, 1957. Won First International Drawing Prize, V° Bienal de São Paulo, 1959. Has illustrated many books since 1959. Resident Mexico City.

PERU

Fernando de Szyszlo
Born 1925, Lima. Attended School of Fine Arts, Catholic University, Lima, 1944–1946. First one-man show, Peruvian-American Cultural Institute, Lima, 1947. Has lived in Europe and New York. Visiting critic, Art Department, College of Architecture, Cornell University, 1962. Participated in several important international exhibitions. Professor of Art, Catholic University, Lima. Resident Lima.

URUGUAY

Joaquín Torres García
Born 1874, Montevideo. Studied with Vinardell, Barcelona, 1891. Studied at Academy of Fine Arts, Barcelona. Moved to New York, 1920. Moved to Paris, 1925. First one-man show, Galerie Fabre, Paris, 1926. Returned to Montevideo, 1934. Died in Montevideo, 1949.

Nelson Ramos
Born 1932, Dolores, Uruguay. Studied at Escuela Nacional de Bellas Artes, Montevideo, 1951. First one-man show, 'Amigos de Arte', Montevideo, 1955. Studied in Brazil with Friedlaender and Camargo, 1959–1961. Returned to Uruguay, 1961. Studied in Spain, 1963. Resident Montevideo.

VENEZUELA

Armando Reverón
Born 1889, Caracas. Studied at Escuela de Artes Plásticas y Artes Aplicadas, 1904. Recipient of fellowship to study in Madrid and Barcelona, 1913. Resident 1921–1954 of small seashore town, Macuto. Died in a sanitarium, 1954.

Alejandro Otero
Born 1921, El Manteco, Venezuela. Studied at Escuela de Artes Plásticas y Artes Aplicadas, Caracas, 1939–1943. First one-man show, Ateneo de Valencia, 1944. Resident France, 1945–1952. Professor, Escuela de Artes Plásticas y Artes Aplicadas, Caracas, 1954–1959. Resident Caracas.

Jesús Rafael Soto
Born 1923, Ciudad Bolívar, Venezuela. Studied at Escuela de Artes Plásticas y Artes Aplicadas, Caracas, 1942–1947. Director, Escuela de Bellas Artes, Maracaibo, 1947–1950. First one-man show, Caracas, 1948. Resident Paris since 1950.

Humberto Jaimes-Sánchez
Born 1930, San Cristóbal. Studied at Escuela de Artes Plásticas y Artes Aplicadas, Caracas, 1947–1950. Studied in Rome and Paris, 1954–1957. One-man exhibition, Pan American Union, Washington, D.C., 1957. Teaches at Escuela de Artes Plásticas y Artes Aplicadas, Caracas. Resident Caracas.

Jacobo Borges
Born 1931, Caracas. Studied at Escuela de Artes Plásticas y Artes Aplicadas, Caracas, 1949. Fellowship to study in Paris, 1952. Honorable mention, IV° Bienal de São Paulo, 1957. Represented in numerous group exhibitions since 1957, including XXIX° Biennale, Venice, 1958. Armando Reverón Bienal Award, Caracas, 1965. Resident Caracas.

BIBLIOGRAPHY

The following is a selective bibliography on contemporary Latin American art prepared by The Solomon R. Guggenheim Museum. It is limited to material recently published, and to the countries represented in the exhibition. The purpose has been to provide a cross section of the literature available on the relatively new topic of contemporary Latin American art. Much of the material cited is in the form of exhibition catalogs, but only catalogs with substantial introductory texts have been included. A few works pertaining to established and well-known artists appear at the end of the bibliography.

GENERAL

Books

Diego A. Iniguez, Marco Dorta, and Mario Buschiazzo. *Historia del arte hispanoamericano*, 3 vols, Barcelona-Madrid, Salvat Editores, 1945–1956.

Robert Smith and Elizabeth Wilder. *A Guide to the Art of Latin America*, Washington, D.C., Hispanic Foundation, Library of Congress, 1948.

Marta Traba. *La pintura nueva en Latinoamérica*, Bogotá, Ediciones Librería Central, 1961.

Articles

Stanton L. Catlin. 'New Vistas in Latin American Art', *Art in America*, New York, Vol. 47, No. 3 (1959), pp. 24–31.

José Gómez-Sicre. 'Trends – Latin America', *Art in America*, New York, Vol. 47, No. 3 (1959), pp. 22–23.

Fernando de Szyszlo. 'Contemporary Latin American Painting: A Brief Survey', *The Art Journal*, New York, Vol. 19, No. 2 (Winter 1959–1960), pp. 134–145.

Thomas M. Messer. 'Pan America: Contemporary Idioms', *Art in America*, New York, Vol. 49, No. 3 (1961), pp. 82–92.

José Gómez-Sicre. 'Meeting in Madrid', *Américas*, Washington, D.C., Pan American Union (September 1963), pp. 30–39.

Rafael Squirru. 'Spectrum of Styles in Latin America', *Art in America*, New York, Vol. 52, No. 1 (February 1964), pp. 81–86.

Thomas M. Messer. 'Oigamos con los ojos', *Life en español*, Chicago, Vol. 24, No. 7 (September 28, 1964), pp. 50–51.

Jorge R. Brest. 'L'Art actuel de l'Amérique latine en Argentine', *Art International*, Zurich, Vol. 8, No. 10 (December 1964), pp. 26–30.

Lawrence Alloway. 'Latin America and International Art', *Art in America*, New York, Vol. 53, No. 3 (1965), pp. 64–77.

The Texas Quarterly (University of Texas, Austin), Vol. 8 (October 1965). Special issue on South American art, with articles by José Gómez-Sicre, Marc Berkowitz, Marta Traba, Clara Diament de Sujo, and others.

Thomas M. Messer. 'Latin America: Esso Salon of Young Artists', *Art in America*, New York, Vol. 53, No. 5 (October–November 1965), pp. 120–121.

Exhibition Catalogs

Dallas Museum of Fine Arts, October 10–November 29, 1959, *South American Art Today*. Catalog introductions by Jerry Bywaters and José Gómez-Sicre.

Institute of Contemporary Art, Boston, 1961, *Latin America–New Departures*. Circulation in the United States, 1961–1962. Catalog introductions by Thomas M. Messer and José Gómez-Sicre.

Palacios de Velázquez y Cristal del Retiro, Madrid, May–June 1963, *Arte de América y España*. Hospital de la Santa Cruz, Barcelona, and Palacio de la Virreina, Barcelona, August–September 1963. Catalog text by Gregorio Marañón, José Pedro Argúl, and others.

Haus der Städtischen Kunstsammlungen, Bonn, June 30–September 1, 1963. Traveled to many German museums in 1964. Among them Akademie der Künste, Berlin, January 12–February 9, 1964, and Staatliche Kunsthalle, Baden-Baden, March 1964. Catalog introductions by Will Grohmann and Paul Westheim.

Galería Bonino, New York, September 21–October 10, 1964, and Museo de Bellas Artes, Mexico City, November 3–15, 1964, *Magnet: New York*. Catalog introductions by Robert M. Wool and Thomas M. Messer.

Museo de Bellas Artes and Ateneo de Caracas, Caracas, January 10–February 10, 1965, *Evaluación de la pintura latinoamericana: Años '60*. Catalog introduction by Thomas M. Messer.

Corcoran Gallery, Washington, D.C., April 1965, *Esso Salon of Young Artists*. Traveling in the United States. Catalog introduction by José Gómez-Sicre.

Musée d'Art Moderne de la Ville de Paris, June 1965, *Artistes latino-américains de Paris*. Catalog introduction by Denys Chevalier.

ARGENTINA

Books

Manuel Mujíca-Lainez. *Argentina*, series 'Art in Latin America Today', Washington, D.C., Pan American Union, 1961.

Articles

Terence Grieder. 'Argentina's New Figurative Art', *The Art Journal*, New York, Vol. 24, No. 1 (Fall 1964), pp. 2–6.

Jan van der Marck. 'New Art of Argentina', *Art International*, Zurich, Vol. 8, No. 8 (October 20, 1964), pp. 35–38.

Exhibition Catalogs

Museo Nacional de Bellas Artes, Buenos Aires, July 1960, *F. Muro, Grilo, Ocampo, Sakai, Testa*. Catalog introduction by Jorge Romero Brest.

— Buenos Aires, 1961, *150 años de arte argentino*. Catalog text by Córdova Iturburu, José León Pagano, and others.

— Buenos Aires, June 15–July 7, 1963, *Deira, Macció, Noé, de la Vega*. Catalog introduction by Jorge Romero Brest.

— Buenos Aires, October–November 1963, *Exposición Phases*. Catalog introductions by Jorge Romero Brest, Julio Llinás, and Edouard Jaguer.

Musée National d'Art Moderne, Paris, December 1963–February 1964, *L'Art argentin actuel*. Catalog preface by Jean Cassou, introduction by G. Kosice.

Walker Art Center, Minneapolis, September 9–October 11, 1964, *New Art of Argentina*. Also Akron Art Institute, Akron, October 25–November 29, 1964. Atlanta Art Association, Atlanta, December 13, 1964–January 17, 1965. The University Art Museum, University of Texas, Austin, February 7–March 14, 1965. Catalog introduction by Jorge Romero Brest.

BRAZIL

Books

Luis de Almeida Cunha. *Brasil I*, series 'Art in Latin America Today', Washington, D.C., Pan American Union, 1960.

Jorge Romero Brest. *La pintura brasileña contemporánea*, Buenos Aires, Editorial Poseidón.

Articles

Martin L. Friedman. 'New Art of Brazil', *Art International*, Zurich, Vol. 6, No. 5–6 (Summer 1962), pp. 113–118.

G. Boudaille. 'Sept Brésiliens de l'École de Paris', *XXᵉ Siècle*, Paris, Vol. 37, No. 22 (December 1963), supp. pp. 41–44.

Mario Barata. 'L'Art actuel au Brésil', *Aujourd'hui*, Paris, Vol. 8, No. 46 (July 1964), pp. 60–63.

Antonio Bento. 'L'Art contemporain au Brésil', *Aujourd'hui*, Paris, Vol. 8, No. 46 (July 1964), pp. 56–57.

J.A. Franca. 'Artistes brésiliens de Paris', *Aujourd'hui*, Paris, Vol. 8, No. 46 (July 1964), pp. 64–67.

Marc Berkowitz. 'Contemporary Brazilian Painting and Printmaking', *Studio International*, London, Vol. 169 (February 1965), pp. 56–63.

Exhibition Catalogs

Walker Art Center, Minneapolis, 1962, *New Art of Brazil*. Traveled to City Art Museum, St Louis; San Francisco Museum of Art, San Francisco; Colorado Springs Fine Arts Center, Colorado Springs, 1962–1963. Catalog introduction by Roberto de Oliveira Campos. Text by Martin L. Friedman.

CHILE

Books

Antonio R. Romera. *Historia de la pintura chilena*, Santiago, Empresa Editora Zig-Zag, 1960.

— *Chile*, series 'Art in Latin America Today', Washington, D.C., Pan American Union, 1963.

COLOMBIA

Books

Marta Traba. *Colombia*, series 'Art in Latin America Today', Washington, D.C., Pan American Union, 1959.

Articles

Marta Traba. 'Pan America: Five Contemporary Colombians', *Art in America*, New York, Vol. 48, No. 1 (1960), pp. 110–111.

— 'Contemporary Art of Colombia', *Art in America*, New York, Vol. 51, No. 2 (1963), pp. 106–107.

— 'Colombia: Year Zero', *Art International*, Zurich, Vol. 9, No. 5 (June 1965), pp. 16–19.

Exhibition Catalogs

Galleria Nazionale d'Arte Moderna, Rome, March–April 1962, *Arte de Colombia*. Catalog introduction by José Gómez-Sicre.

Liljevalchs Konsthall, Stockholm, April 27–May 20, 1962, *Colombiansk Konst*. Catalog introduction by José Gómez-Sicre.

MEXICO

Books

Mackinley Helm. *Modern Mexican Painters*, New York, Harper and Brothers, 1941.

Alfaro D. Siqueiros. *El muralismo de México*, México, Ediciones Mexicanas, 1950.

Justino Fernández. *Arte moderno y contemporáneo de México*, México, D.F., Universidad Nacional de México, 1952.

Bernard S. Myers. *Mexican Painting in Our Time*, New York, Oxford University Press, 1956.

Luis Cordoza y Aragón. *México: pintura activa*, México, D.F., Ediciones Era, S.A., 1961.

Jean Charlot. *The Mexican Mural Renaissance, 1920–1925*, New Haven, Yale University Press, 1963.

Articles

J.A. Franca. 'La jeune peinture mexicaine', *Aujourd'hui*, Paris, Vol. 7, No. 39 (November 1962), pp. 18–19.

S. Rodman. 'What's Mexican in Mexican Art?' *Art in America*, New York, Vol. 51, No. 3 (June 1963), pp. 116–119.

James Harithas. 'Phoenix Art Museum Show Points Trends in Mexican Art Today', *The Art Gallery*, Connecticut, Vol. 8, No. 5 (February 1965), pp. 32–39. Exhibition review.

Exhibition Catalogs

Traveled in France to Bordeaux, Paris, Lille, Lyon, and Toulouse, 1958, *Art mexicain contemporain*. Catalog introductions by Miguel Salas Anzures, Jaime Torres Bodet, and others.

Phoenix Art Museum, December 12, 1964–February 15, 1965, *Contemporary Mexican Artists*. Catalog introduction by James Harithas.

VENEZUELA

Books

Clara Diament de Sujo. *Venezuela*, series 'Art in Latin America Today', Washington, D.C., Pan American Union, 1962.

Articles

Clara Diament de Sujo. 'Living in Painting: Venezuelan Art Today', *Art International*, Lugano, Vol. 9, No. 3 (April 1965), pp. 34–37.

Exhibition Catalogs

Museo de Bellas Artes, Caracas, April 19–July 5, 1961, *Pintura venezolana 1661–1961*. Catalog text by Guillermo Menses.

Instituto Cultural Venezolano–Israelí, New York, March 15–31, 1962, *17 Venezuelan Painters*. Text by Miguel C. Arroyo.

Museo de Arte Moderno, Bogotá, June 18–July 8, 1963, *Pintura contemporánea venezolana*. Statements by Miguel Arroyo, Hans Neumann, Clara Diament de Sujo, and others.

INDIVIDUAL ARTISTS

JOAQUÍN TORRES GARCÍA (Uruguay)

Writings by Torres García

Joaquín Torres García. *Universalismo constructivo*, Buenos Aires, Editorial Poseidón, 1944.

MATTA (Chile)

Monographs

William Rubin. *Matta*, Museum of Modern Art Bulletin, New York, Vol. 25, No. 1 (1957), pp. 3–36.

Books illustrated by Matta

André Breton. *Arcane 17*, New York, Brentano's, 1944.

Writings by Matta

with Katherine S. Dreier. *Duchamp's Glass...an Analytical Reflection*, New York, Société Anonyme, 1944.

JOSÉ LUIS CUEVAS (Mexico)

Monographs

Philippe Soupault. *La personnalité de Cuevas*, series 'Collection d'artistes de ce temps', Michel Brien, Paris, 1955.

— and Horacio Flores-Sánchez. *Le peintre José Luis Cuevas*, series 'Collection d'artistes de ce temps', Michel Brien, Paris, 1955.

Books Illustrated by Cuevas

The Worlds of Kafka and Cuevas, Philadelphia, Falcon Press, 1959. Texts by José Gómez-Sicre, Max Brod, and Rollo May, and quotations from Franz Kafka text.

Manuel Moreno Jimeno. *Las citas*, Lima, Peru, 1960.

William Macleod. *The Ends of Legend's String*, Washington, D.C., Views Associates Press, 1960.

José Luis Cuevas. *Recollections of Childhood: Twelve Original Lithographs with a Text by the Artist*, Los Angeles, Kanthos Press, 1962.

Alberto Cuevas-Novelo. *El alma y el cerebro*, México, D.F., 1962.

RUFINO TAMAYO (Mexico)

Monographs

Robert J. Goldwater. *Rufino Tamayo*, New York, Quadrangle Press, 1947.

Justino Fernández. *Rufino Tamayo*, México, D.F., Imprenta Universitaria, 1948.

Enrique F. Gual. *Drawings by Tamayo*, México, D.F., Ediciones Mexicanas, S.A., 1950.

Raymond Cogniat. *Rufino Tamayo*, series 'Collection d'artistes de ce temps', Paris, Presses Littéraires de France, 1951.

Paul Westheim. *Tamayo*, México, D.F., Ediciones Artes de México, 1957.